THE EGO'S CODE

- UNDERSTAND THE TRUTH BEHIND YOUR NEGATIVITY!

For my girls...
May all your dreams come true!

THE
EGO'S
CODE

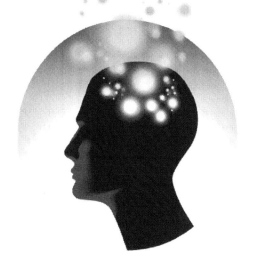

Understand the truth behind your negativity!
Learn how to decipher your code…
…and stop sabotaging your success!

CLAYTON JOHN AINGER

THE EGO'S CODE
UNDERSTAND THE TRUTH BEHIND YOUR NEGATIVITY!

First published in 2015 by
Panoma Press Ltd
48 St Vincent Drive, St Albans, Herts, AL1 5SJ UK
info@panomapress.com
www.panomapress.com

Cover design/Illustrations by Michael Inns
Artwork by Karen Gladwell

ISBN 978-1-909623-95-8

This book is available online and in all good bookstores.

Contents

EXERCISES

What you are feeling is real, right,
important... and has meaning!

Preface

IT IS my pleasure to welcome you to the Ego's Code.

I have learned over the years that there are no coincidences and that in hindsight everything happens for a reason until you stop living in your past. Yes, like you, I have experienced challenges, hardship and negativity, sometimes to the point of incapacitation. Would I change the challenges that I have experienced, the hardships I have overcome, and the negativity I have endured? Absolutely not, because what I have experienced in my life has helped me to design who I am today and the life I choose to live. However, what I recognized is that the challenges, the hardships, and the negativity went on a lot longer than was necessary, because even though I intellectually knew better, I did not do better, by making the necessary changes in my life when I could have. I kept on playing out what seemed like the same scenarios in my life. It was like I was a zombie living in a trance.

Life is here to be lived, through our experiences, good and bad, and by definition you will experience adversity, challenges, hardship and negativity, but you are not meant to "live in it." Life leaves clues and patterns so that you can quickly get the learning from the 'negative' experience and use it to experience more happiness and joy in life. Unfortunately, sometimes we all become consumed, and lost in the mire, the heaviness and unhappiness. What if I could help you to identify the patterns and clues in your challenges, your hardships, and your negativity, so that you use this to experience more happiness and joy? In a nutshell, that is what you will learn in this book.

Your patterns are everywhere... you just have to notice them.

There are patterns to help you enjoy life, patterns to help you grow, patterns to help you find a great job, patterns to help you find your soul mate, patterns to help you with money problems, patterns to keep you safe... there are even patterns to your self-talk, in your thoughts, your feelings, your emotions, and your behaviors...

Why? Because they have meaning!

So many of us walk around in a trance, missing out on so much of the beauty around us, not allowing that beauty to touch our hearts. More importantly, we miss out on the magic within us because we don't notice, we ignore, or worse, we fear, the patterns, signs and signals presented to us that are meant to help us.

Only yesterday, my friend sent me a short video clip about how our thoughts are things that shape our reality. In the video, the presenter said, we have on average 60,000 thoughts per day and the majority are negative, therefore you need to be careful what you think. I have a different view. What if the reason you experience 60,000 **repetitive** negative thoughts (plus the negativity feelings, emotions, behaviors and self-talk associated with those thoughts) is because you don't notice the patterns in your thoughts, feelings, emotions, behaviors, and self-talk and you don't do something about it. I know from my own life, when we start to notice what is actually going on and decipher its meaning the negativity disappears, and your life changes for the better. You do have a choice - you could carefully box away your negativity and be very careful to focus on enjoying more positive ones, BUT, and it's a big BUT, I promise you they will come back, and when they do, it will be with a vengeance, until you do pay attention and you will continue to sabotage rather than live your life as it is meant to be lived – in harmony, in truth, full of fun, learning, growth, imagination, creativity, happiness, love and excessive joy!

In this book I am going to help you understand the truth behind your patterns and how to decipher your unique code hidden in your thoughts, your feelings, your emotions, your behaviors... and the things you say to yourself in secret.

First a few important things I want you to know.

This book is **your book** for you to use as you see fit. It is full of exercises, personal stories about me, my family, friends, clients (all of whom I have changed the names to protect their anonymity), mini rune readings and animal spirits to guide you.

You can read your book from cover to cover, dip in and out, or use it for your daily wisdom by opening the book at random. Any and all approaches will help you. Please do what is right for you.

The Exercises

When I run my events, I frequently use exercises to bring the teaching alive even more. Each session of teaching is accompanied or followed immediately by a relevant exercise, and when necessary, an introduction to the runes and power animals. This is often the most effective way to embed learning and move participants from intellectualizing a theory to making it operational in their life. In this book I have followed the same pattern.

What are runes? *Runes were used as a method of communication across Scandinavia from around the 3rd Century to 13th Century. Today runes are used as a tool for divination. A rune is like a little stone with a symbol inscription. Each symbol has a specific energy and meaning to help you in life.*

When doing the exercises in this book, you can use the energy of the runes to help you achieve your goals. You can use the energy of the runes in two ways.

1. **Close your eyes, focus on the symbol and its meaning, whilst repeating the name of the rune out loud or**

2. **You can draw the symbol of the rune on a piece of paper and carry it around with you in your pocket.**

What are Power Animals? Power Animals act similar to a Guardian Angel. They are a helping spirit that is essential for success. Everyone has power animals that help guide him or her through life, to protect them from illness, and increase their personal power. Each Power Animal has a different wisdom and gift to share with you on your life's journey.

Similarly to the runes, when you are working through the exercises in this book you can also work with the Power Animals. The best way to do this is to close your eyes and pretend you are the animal in its natural habitat or pretend you are riding on the back of the animal. I would also invite you to get to know each of the animals even better by doing your own research. In my experience, the more you know about an animal, the better the results you will get. I have also been known to print off pictures and have them on my desk when working.

Each exercise immediately comes after the related teaching. To get the most benefit from this book, I recommend you do each exercise as you come to it.

I would recommend that you keep a note book nearby in which you can write your responses and learning from each exercise as you come to it, together with your thoughts, feelings, emotions, etc. positive and negative. This will help you to learn about you in the most effective way.

Please, please, please do not be scared or worried about negativity coming up. Just make a note of it, say thank you, and move on. This is all part of the process of getting to a state where you can live your true life, in truth.

How to maximize your results from this book

- **Please keep an open mind!**

  As you read this book, you will see, feel, experience things that are a little different! Please try them on for size. If they work for you, great! There will be many options. Some you will use, others you may grow into and some you may park for now and use later.

- **Play full out**

  As you work your way through this book, give 100% in everything you do! You may surprise yourself.

- **Challenge yourself!**

  Expect more from you than anyone else would expect! In life, we tend to do more for others than we do for ourselves – so give yourself the same gift you give to others – give 100% of you, to you.

- **Ground yourself and use the material**

  So many people read books, such as this, and never use what they have learned. Choose to be different! The more you work with the content, the better your results will be!

- **Have fun!**

  Laugh, play and have some fun today and everyday!

- **Be true to yourself!**

  Listen to your heart, trust your intuition and be true to who you really are!

How the book is laid out

Your book is laid out in three parts. The teaching shared in your book builds up progressively, it is layered and sometimes appears repetitive. This is done purposely so that each section and its respective content builds on what has gone before it.

Part One is about *raising your awareness* and understanding what is going on, not only inside but also in the patterns and clues outside from your surroundings, and the people whom you interact with. **Part Two** focuses on *aligning to your truth*. We specifically explore the 8 truths to decipher your ego's code. **Part Three** are bite size chapters about *living your truth* every day.

Finally, a very wise man once said to me, "be curious first and critical second."

As you read your book, be open, be curious and be aware of your negativity e.g. I can't, but, etc. because it will help you decipher your code.

Then, as the same wise man said, "Be prepared to surrender who you 'think' you are and step into the 'truth' of who you really are. Truly notice what is going on inside. Ask yourself, 'How would I choose to make things different in my life, if this is my truth?'"

The Ego's Code

EVERY DAY we all experience negativity whether it be feelings, emotions, actions, behavior or self-talk within ourselves or from others. For many people it causes them to sabotage success, relationships, health, wellbeing and finances, ultimately preventing them from fully experiencing their life and living their dreams.

How do I know? Because this was me...

In my own life I have regularly experienced such intense negativity. I sabotaged my success, my weight, my health and vitality, my relationships, my career, my finances and my spirituality.

Let me share a few examples with you...

Regarding my **health and weight**. I used to weigh 252 pounds. I remember working in London and having a full English breakfast of sausages, bacon, eggs, beans, fried bread and French fries every day for nine months. Then, at lunchtime having foods like pasta, and in the evening, going out with colleagues drinking until I would fall into my apartment. Today, I am proud to say that I weigh a healthy 182 pounds and have for the majority of the past 10 years.

Regarding my **career and finances**. I used to be an accountant and tax consultant, but for 10 years I was so unhappy and felt unfulfilled. I left with no money and high debts to start my own consultancy business, which I have grown to a six-figure turnover that is now on course for seven figures.

Regarding my **relationships**. I went from being divorced and alone to being happily married to my twin flame soul mate.

Regarding my **spirituality**. I was so afraid of what people would think and say about me that I hid my gifts for years. I have experienced psychic attacks from other so called "teachers" who tried to get me to stop. I now give psychic readings to people all over the world. I run spiritual events and here I am writing my first book, *The Ego's Code.*

I am very comfortable in my own skin and I have accepted who I am and all that I am as a limitless being. I play many roles in my life – husband, father, son, brother, friend, entrepreneur, business owner, health nut, shaman, psychic medium, speaker, author just to name a few – and I love them all!

So what is the Ego's Code?

There are patterns to your negativity. It has meaning! That is why the same things keep happening over and over again!

There is something fundamental that you need to learn that will help you in your life, to heal some aspect(s) of your life that you are unhappy with! The combination of your negative self-talk, thoughts, feelings, actions, behaviors and emotional wellbeing highlight a key that will help you to understand and decipher their meaning so that you can eventually *live an Ego free identity*. **This is called the Ego's Code.**

Introduction

Through the "I" to the "One"

HOW YOU live and choose to behave in your life, and the actions or non-action you take impacts on the life of others and the world around you, whether you like it or not. As I have learned in my own life there are *always* consequences, good and bad, that directly or indirectly affect those around me.

The challenge is, as studies have shown, in our mind we only truly see the immediate impact on our life, those closest to us, or in our immediate community. Generally, society focuses on the question and base decisions on "what it means to me", which makes it easier to dismiss the effect of actions on those further away. As a result, we never or hardly ever actually see the consequences, the impact or even the benefits our actions have on those people around the world because of the physical "distance" from our own reality or because we say to ourselves "I am just one person, what harm can I do or help can I give?"

Consider for one moment, Lehman Bros. Lehman Bros, the 158 year old company run by former CEO Dick Fuld, collapsed under the weight of bad investments and sent a tidal wave of panic through the global financial system resulting in billions in government bailouts, near collapse of the nation's financial systems, slowed economic growth, high unemployment and hesitant consumers. Do you think that Dick Fuld and other similar Wall Street bankers thought about the wider impact of the decisions they were making?

There is a concept called the *six degrees of separation,* which suggests that one person is no more than six steps away from each person on Earth. It therefore follows that our behavior, pro-active or reactive, has an affect directly or indirectly on every person on Earth.

> *The Six Degrees of Separation* is the theory that everyone and everything is six or fewer steps away, by way of introduction, from any other person in the world, so that a chain of "a friend of a friend" can be made to connect any two people in a maximum of six steps.

When I pause in my life for a moment and look at the world around us, I see so much beauty, so much grace, so much splendor and so much happiness; but I also see the negativity that consumes us and surrounds us every day; pain and despair, death and destruction, and illness, all of which is reported daily on the television and in the newspapers.

What I also realize like many others is that I have contributed to the way the world is today. Furthermore, I recognize that small changes or variations in my own behavior can produce large beneficial changes or variations in the behavior of others for the long term. This is also known as *"the butterfly effect"*. The phrase refers to the idea that when a butterfly flaps its wings it creates tiny changes in the atmosphere that may ultimately alter the path of a tornado or delay, accelerate or even prevent the occurrence of a tornado in another location. The flapping wing represents a small change, which causes a chain of events leading to a large-scale alteration of events. Had the butterfly not flapped its wings (or the individual taken alternate action), the outcome may have been vastly different.

> *The butterfly effect* is the term used to describe how small changes to a seemingly unrelated object, situation or system, can affect large complex systems, meaning that the tiniest influence on one part of a system can have a huge effect on another part.

The world as you know it is changing. Over the next 10 years you will not recognize the world in which you live today. If you look carefully, the signs are already here. People in society are no longer sitting back and following blindly. They are beginning to reawaken and to realize that if something is to change, the change must begin with them.

For example, people are questioning:

- The intention and integrity behind the actions of our business leaders and world leaders

- The demands on their time from employers who expect more and more from us with longer working hours for less pay and shorter breaks
- The quality of relationships that surround us every day
- The drains on our time, energy, money etc.

Maybe you are asking yourself the same questions.

But where and how do you begin?

Today, we all want more and expect more out of life: To have "quality" of life! To "feel" alive! To be happy and ultimately fulfilled!

The thing is that most of us don't have any real clarity or understanding about what happiness is or what living a fulfilled life means to us as individuals. We have some ideas about what we *think* it means e.g. more time for fun and play, a romantic relationship with a soul-mate, to have a job we are passionate about, to have a lot of money, to have a big house, a fast car, etc., but no real clarity, or understanding, otherwise we would already be living our fulfilled life.

What we do have, from our life experiences, are the feelings and emotions of what we *think* happiness feels like – excitement, exuberance, exhilaration, laughing for so long that your breath is taken away, a feeling that nothing can stop you, like you are almost flying!

Whatever these feelings mean to you, they have a tendency to be short lived. One minute you feel amazing, you are flying high, full of energy, full of laughter, everything you touch turns to gold and the next minute you have crashed and you are consumed by doubt, worry, fear, anxiety, negativity and you don't understand why.

So many people in the world feel unhappy or distressed with certain or all areas of their life causing them to feel tired, often exhausted, sometimes angry, confused, frustrated, miserable, stressed and even depressed. They feel trapped and unable to move forward. Sometimes there can be so many things they feel unhappy about that they don't know which way to turn, where to start or what to do first.

What's great is that they know and feel that there must be something more to life than what they already have or what they are living and experiencing. In fact, they know there is a purpose to their life but because they are focusing on what's missing or consumed by negativity they just can't put their finger on it. So they just keep doing the same old things over and over again, day after day, spending time dwelling on the same old crap, living in the past, staying in a job they hate, being in a relationship with someone they don't love, living a life that does not fulfill them. Until one day they look at themselves in the mirror and life has passed them by...

Or maybe that is your biggest fear – that life will pass you by. You want to be happy and fulfilled so much that you keep searching and searching, looking for answers, for that magic bullet or pill that will transform your life overnight, with the least effort because you are so tired. You attend personal development workshop after workshop, read book after book, change your jobs over and over again, change careers, change relationships bouncing from partner to partner. But nothing really changes.

Or maybe to the outside world you appear to have everything – the perfect career, successful company, big house, fast car, beautiful partner, so much money you can buy whatever you want and yet you still feel unhappy and unfulfilled.

The challenge is you don't understand why you feel this way or do the things you do, so the cycle begins again. You continue searching, continue looking for answers, not really knowing what you are looking for, making change after change, not knowing why and buying everything you want to fill an empty void, and just for a short while you feel great for that brief moment in time, then that feeling begins to drift away and once again you feel lost, out of sorts, out of balance... empty inside, knowing that something is missing.

How do I know all this? Because this was me!

I have sabotaged my success several times in an attempt to prevent my life from changing, and avoid being the real me, someone who lives his truth. Maybe the time was not right, maybe I was not ready in terms of where I was on my journey, whatever I do or however I try to justify my reasons, the truth is there are only excuses. The simple truth is: "*I stopped myself from fully experiencing the best of who I am and the best of my life.*" But the questions remain, how did I unravel the mystery of who I am? How did I remain focused long enough to make a sustainable lasting change? How did I realize the truth of who I am so I could start living a life that is true to my heart?

These questions bring about many other questions – How did I create the reality I was living? Why did I experience negative feelings and emotions? Why did I procrastinate? Why was I so harsh on myself? Why did I cause myself so much emotional harm and tell myself so many negative and disempowering things? Why did I lie to myself? Why did I lie to others? Why did I create the masks I lived behind for so long? Why did I experience a feeling of numbness and separateness? Why did I detach myself from my life and from those I love? Why was I choosing to merely exist and play small rather than experience the very best of who I am and all my life has to offer?

Have you ever asked yourself the same or similar questions and wondered why you do some of the things you do? I will answer all these questions in this book.

Looking back what I realize is that everything was happening for a reason, despite it not feeling or appearing that way at the time. What I can tell you is that everything unfolded in a perfect and extraordinary way; a way that was totally unexpected and yet had such grace, finesse, order and was better than expected. A way that was so simple that in the beginning I did not see the signs, the signals, the patterns, or the answers that were right in front of me all along. If I had only had the space and awareness to see them earlier to understand their messages I may not have experienced the challenges, the heartache, the pain, the fear, and the stress for as long as I did. If only someone had been there to shine a light on how to see the patterns and how to find the answers. Well these are just some of the reasons why I have written this book.

No matter how you feel at this very moment, about you, your life, your relationships, or your career, please realize that where you are right now is the place you are meant to be. The fact that you have picked up this book indicates you recognize and you realize there is something missing, something out of sync or out of balance in your life. Something may feel wrong, but please note: there is nothing wrong in your life. What you are experiencing is a readiness to progress your life forward to step into the truth of who you are. This may feel daunting or even exciting because you are no longer prepared to *"settle"* and/or to *"put up with"* the way you experience and live your life any longer. In fact this is a time for celebration!

Again, I am going to re-emphasize that where you are in your life right now is the place you are meant to be. You may feel challenged by or struggle with this statement because of the way your life is or how you feel, but ask yourself this question - do you *consciously* get out of bed in the morning and decide – *"Hey, today I am going to feel like crap?"* or *"Today, I am going to beat myself up"* or *"Hey I know, today I am going to sabotage my successful business, relationship or career?"* No of course you don't!

So why does this happen?

In this book, I am going to explain to you the important reason why these things happen, because as you will soon realize, everything happens for a very good reason. Furthermore, I will show you how you can use the negative patterns in your thoughts, feelings, emotions, behaviors and self-talk, to live your life filled with even more happiness.

So why have I entitled my introduction *Through the "I" to the "One"*?

The reason goes back to the opening paragraphs of this introduction and about how we positively change the world in which we live.

Consider the following question. When you feel happy and joyous in your life, how do you treat other people? Are you kind? Even more patient? Considerate? Understanding? Supportive? Helpful? Loving? I know you are answering "yes." I would go one step further and say that is what you do just for starters. Ultimately, when things are going well for you, it is your unconscious desire to help others to feel as great as you do. What is even more incredible is that you do this without an agenda. It is *totally unconditional.*

If I am able to help you see your beauty and experience the awe and wonderment of who you are, to live the life your heart desires, then I know (as a by-product) you will *unconditionally* share the feelings that come with this with all those people you are in contact with. And guess what? They too will pass it forward, *again unconditionally.* It's like a positive virus affecting our world in a positive way. Joy being spread from one person to another. What an incredible and selfless gift that will be. Can you imagine the *real impact* and effect on our world as we know it?

It all starts with you!

So let's begin...

"To know others is intelligence
Knowing yourself is the dawn of genuine wisdom
The mastery of others requires strength
Mastering yourself is true power"

Lao Tse Tao Te Ching, Versus 53 and 81

PART ONE:

RAISING YOUR AWARENESS

- WHAT'S REALLY GOING ON?

Understand the truth behind your negativity!

Learn how to decipher your code…
…and stop sabotaging your success!

Who Are You When You Are Being You?

THERE ARE many messages out in the world today that say there is a 'real you' 'a true you' or a 'divine you,' but let me be very clear... you are not a collection of parts. There is just you! And you are all these things! You are real, you are true, and you are divine! The 'you in you' is more than enough! You are all you need! You are powerful! You are magnificent! You are connected to ALL THINGS, EVERYWHERE! And when you are tapped in, turned on, switched on, connected to you... boy oh boy, look out world here you come! And I know with every cell in my body at some time in your life already you have experienced the true power... that is you. The challenge is consistency and how do you maintain it because sometimes you are up flying high, and other times you are down.

Your life will present you with twists and turns, and I want to assure you that when you experience your best days and when you experience your worst days, the you that is within you is *always* there and is *always* shining bright. No matter what you experience in your life, this fact is *very important* to remember. It is like your own internal flame. When you experience your best days, your internal flame is burning so bright; even when you experience your worst days, your internal flame is still burning bright. You don't feel it or sense it as much because your mind, your head, and your body are in the clouds or focusing on other things. And yet your internal flame continues to burn bright. It is always there for you to access and enjoy. Just remember, even when the weather is miserable outside your window, if you fly high enough into the sky, above the clouds the sun is always there shining bright. Even when it is dark at night, the sun is still shining bright somewhere in our world! It is the same for you.

> **What is your internal flame?** *Your internal flame is all the goodness, the greatness and the positivity that makes you who you are. It is your joy, your passion, your love, your kindness and the divinity within you.*

As you read this book and work through the exercises, it is important for you to understand how you would describe yourself and how you experience you 'in life' when you are *being you.* You can start this by completing **Exercise 1** opposite.

4

Who Am I When I Am Being Me?

Please reflect on the following eight questions and answer each one in as much detail as possible being as clear and honest as you can, expressing the best of you. This will give you a simple benchmark to work with as you progress through this book. The questions are specifically designed to be pondering questions.

EXERCISE 1

1   **What am I doing when I experience the greatest sense of personal fulfilment?**

_____

_____

_____

2   **What am I doing when I experience the greatest sense of joy, peace and happiness?**

_____

_____

_____

3   **Consider my answers to 1 and 2 above, what am I *thinking* <u>before</u> I start what I am doing?**

_____

_____

_____

EXERCISE 1

4 Describe what it *feels* like to be this person:

_____

_____

_____

5 Describe the things *I say to myself,* when I am being this person:

_____

_____

_____

6 Describe the visual images I see when I am being this person:

_____

_____

_____

7 How do I hold and carry my body? How do I walk when I am being this person?

_____

_____

_____

8 **Describe the way I am with other people, when I am being this person:**

_____

_____

_____

There are 168 hours in a week. Allowing 8 hours per night for sleep leaves 112 hours (16 hours per day). In 112 hours how many hours do you experience you (or degrees of you) this way?

Write your approximate answer here ● ● ● ● ● ● ● ▶

How do you feel the rest of the time?
Write your answer in the space below.

_____

_____

Approximately, how many hours each week do you feel this way? ● ● ● ● ● ● ● ▶

Something to think about... or do something about!

7

When I do this exercise on my events, there is often a massive imbalance between the amount of time people spend enjoying things we love, with the people we love compared to doing what they think they *should* do, often to please other people.

There is also a disproportionate imbalance between the amount of time when people feel joyful, happy and fulfilled, compared to when they feel negative. To be specific people feel more negative for more of the time (specifically between 60% and 90% of the time).

This leads us very nicely into the next chapter when we will be exploring what is negativity, is it a bad thing, what is its purpose and where it comes from.

Your Negativity *and*
The Ego's Code

AS A result of the last chapter you now have some awareness about who you are when you are in your groove and in flow; how much time on average you experience feeling great when you are in your groove and how much time on average you feel out of sync.

In this chapter we are going to begin our exploration of Negativity and the reasons why you feel out of sync. It is my intention to raise your awareness of the four important areas below, create a foundation of knowledge for us to build on in later chapters, where I will add more details.

1. **What is Negativity?**

2. **Is it a bad thing?**

3. **What is its purpose?**

4. **Where does it come from?**

What is Negativity?

In the first instance, 'Negativity' is a natural and normal psychological and physical message from your mind and body - a thought, a feeling, an emotion, an action, a behavior or self-talk - letting you know that something is not quite right or how you believe it should be. Its primary purpose is to keep you safe. On a psychological and physical level, the negativity you experience today is an evolution of man's normal and natural 'fight, flight or freeze' responses. But there is so much more to negativity as you will shortly discover...

> *What is a fight, flight or freeze response?* This is
> a physiological reaction that occurs in response to
> a perceived harmful event, attack or threat to our
> survival. The principle states that the animal instinct
> within us reacts to threats with a general discharge
> of our sympathetic nervous system, priming us for
> fighting or fleeing.

Is Negativity a bad thing?

Before I answer the question, I invite you to first notice your immediate response to this question.

When I ask this same question on my events and with my corporate clients, 99 times out of 100, people answer the question with a 'yes'. *Always*, my challenge back, is that if we answer 'yes', then we are making something that is natural and normal - wrong.

So why do we make negativity bad or wrong? Often it is because of the kneejerk or unplanned *reaction* we take (often out of our awareness) and the subsequent outcomes or impact our reactions have on us emotionally and on our lives, e.g., we can feel regret or guilt for hours, weeks, months or even years afterwards.

However, when our *reactions* keep us safe we receive a different internal communication that says everything is as it should be; harmony is restored and therefore it is a good thing. But is it? What if our reaction maintains the status quo and keeps us in an abusive relationship or prevents you from experiencing the best of you in your life, e.g., by embarking on a new career or moving to a new country. Is it good then?

Or it causes harm to you through self-punishment (e.g. over eating) or unkindness (e.g. beating yourself up) or self-sabotage (e.g. by spending money you had put aside to pay your mortgage)?

Or it causes harm to others, which we often see in the world around us and hear from people we know every day? The obvious answer is of course not. But, whilst on a physical level you receive a confirmation that all is as it should be; on a spiritual level we know we should have *responded* differently.

In my experience, the main reason this continues to happen is that over time we have been conditioned and programmed to react in a certain way, which creates a pattern of reactions when certain external or internal buttons are pushed. My concern is that this will continue until we, as a global society, seek and truly understand why we experience negativity or its true purpose. Don't get me wrong, scientists fundamentally understand the biology behind negativity. Neuroscience absolutely understands the brain and body responses, and a lot of philosophers have tried to understand its true meaning. However, if we knew better, surely we would do better, right? We would not react or repeat unhealthy patterns of behavior just to maintain the status quo. We would be living our dreams every day!

What is its purpose?

We all experience negativity. Whether it is through thoughts, feelings, emotions, actions, behaviors or self-talk, it is part of the current human experience and it does have an impact on your life. What matters is the meaning you give it, and then what you do with it when it shows up. Do you give it a bad meaning, stuff it down inside, hoping it will never rear its head again? Do you ignore it and put on a brave face, hoping it will go away? Or do you give it a positive meaning, embrace it and then seek to understand it?

At the start of my events, I have found that the majority of participants do one of two things: stuff it down or ignore it hoping it will go away. In fact, one of the best stories I have heard was from a lady who put a negative situation and associated feelings in a box, wrapped it up as a present, with a big beautiful bow, visualized herself tying chains around it with huge boulders on the end of each chain and threw it in the ocean hoping it would sink to the bottom. Guess what? It did not stay down for long because you cannot hide from it, dissolve it, ignore it, or stuff it down. Why? Because *spiritually,* negativity is not negative it has a purpose! This is why positive thinking does not counteract negativity in the long term. This is why, for example, when you want to lose weight you put it back on again! This is why you continue to sabotage similar events in your life. This is why when you want to sit and write a book, you procrastinate, as I did for so long!

Negativity is energy and all the different forms of negativity have their own unique energetic signature, frequency and vibration. The great thing about energy is that it can be changed, released or transformed into something that will serve you rather than incapacitate or hinder you. So, if you change the meaning and name of the negativity from something that is bad to something that is natural and here to help you to learn from, watch what happens! Crazy, I know, especially when it makes you feel so bad. I promise that when you start to do this and the more you do, you will see evidence of the change in your life too! It will transform on all levels.

Where does negativity come from?

The most important thing you need to understand about negativity is that ALL forms of negativity, and I mean ALL negativity, are echoes or whispers of your past, i.e. they relate to and come from events in your past. Not just your past in your current life time, but your past in your previous lifetimes, too!

So, every time you experience a negative thought, feeling, emotion, action, behavior or self-talk, you are reliving an event from your past, in the here and now. Basically your mind and your body have a perfect memory of your life experiences and you are unconsciously reliving a past experience.

This is why, even when life is going great, you are flying high and feeling unstoppable and all of a sudden something happens, a triggering event, and you feel like you are back where you started! In my life it used to feel like "Groundhog

Day", where I was reliving the same event over and over again, just with different people or a similar situation. I continued to attract people and situations into my life so that I could play out my past over and over again.

But how can a past life experience be experienced in your current life?

Past life negativity

As I said above, *spiritually*, negativity is not negative. It is energy that needs to be released or transformed, but how does that energy get there in the first place and how do you release it?

Let me explain.

Every soul is on a 'learning journey.' *Everyone* in life, has two or three core fundamental lessons they need to learn – it may be about money, relationships, self-worth, love, career, health, appreciation, gratitude, etc. There are a whole host of things and what I know to be true is that *they will be specific to you.* e.g. my core life lessons are to feel safe in my spiritual teachings and to keep others safe that are on the journey with me, to feel worthy of receiving, to feel love, and not to fear wealth, but to accept financial abundance into my life.

All life lessons and negativity relate to traumas in your past lives and from the past in your current life time. As you will find out below there is a link and a relationship between the two.

Every time you experienced a trauma of any kind, on a scale *(see illustration 1)* from minor (e.g. someone shouting at you to the point you feel scared) to severe (e.g. being raped or murdered) it creates a tear or hole in your soul and part of your soul leaves.

IMPACT ON YOUR SOUL

MINOR		SEVERE
RIP/CUT	TEAR	HOLE
SHOCK	WOUND	TRAUMA
eg. SHOUTING	eg. BURNED	eg. MURDERED

Illustration 1 - *Trauma Scale*

The piece of soul that leaves goes to a place in the consciousness where it feels safe. This is why so often people I work with say, "I just feel something is missing" or "I feel I have lost part of me." As a shamanic practitioner, I see and experience the consciousness as a "World Tree", with three levels: the lower *shadow* world, middle world (*the here and now*), and the upper world (*our connection to divinity*).

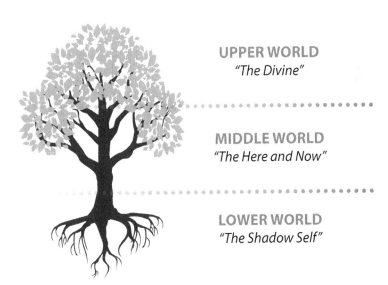

UPPER WORLD
"The Divine"

MIDDLE WORLD
"The Here and Now"

LOWER WORLD
"The Shadow Self"

Illustration 2 - *World Tree*

I will be talking in more detail about the World Tree in the Chapter on '8 Truths to Decipher Your Code' on page 134.

On a soul level, the tear or hole creates a 'void' and into the void goes all the negativity – thoughts, feelings, emotions, actions, behaviors and self-talk associated with that trauma.

It is from here that the Ego is created. Yes, created!

Before I continue, let me ask you two questions. When someone dies, what happens to his or her soul? Yes... it leaves the physical body and transcends. *Every* person I ask, *every* time replies with this answer or something similar. So here is my second question... what happens to the *Ego,* because we all have one?

It is at this point, I want to give thanks and acknowledge a good friend of mine, Paul Cobley. Paul died a number of years ago, and it was when I visited him in the Chapel of Rest that he gave me this answer. When someone dies his or her Ego also leaves the body and transcends, in fact it goes home. It reconnects with their divine Higher Self. Whaaaat? I will pause for a moment and let what I have just shared with you sink in. The Higher Self and the ego are one and the same. How is this possible?

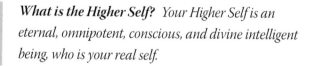

What is the Higher Self? *Your Higher Self is an eternal, omnipotent, conscious, and divine intelligent being, who is your real self.*

Let me explain.

At the point of incarnation, i.e. when you begin your current lifetime something magical and wonderful happens –

Your Higher Self splits in two – into your divine Higher Self and your Ego. Your Higher Self becomes omnipresent and is everywhere, and your Ego Self enters your physical body and mind. We will talk about the specific characteristics of each in more detail later. For now, what you need to understand is that your Ego becomes programmed with all your past life lessons, trauma and negativity and your Higher Self contains the solutions to your life lessons, trauma and negativity. This difference is very significant as you will find out shortly.

As you embark on your life's journey, your Ego attracts to you situations and people so that you can learn and release the negative energy. The whole purpose of which is to heal the tear or hole in your soul so that you can become whole again! But as we have already discussed above, we have been conditioned to give negativity a bad meaning and stuff it down inside, hoping it will never rear its head again or ignore it and we wonder why the same things keep happening over and over again.

If you consider the meaning of Ego to be:

> **E**xpand your
> **G**reatness
> **O**ut

When you experience wholeness you are really experiencing the joy of your Ego returning home and reconnecting with your divine Higher Self. Please, please, please hear me when I say you can absolutely experience wholeness during your life… you do *not* have to wait until you die! In other words, your Ego completely disappears and you live in the truth, your truth! The only reason you have an ego is because of the trauma you experienced in the past, so when you heal the trauma and release the energy, your Ego has done its job!

Therefore the reason your life is challenging in one or more areas or is not changing is because when you stuff your negativity down or ignore it, you are unconsciously sending a message out to your Ego and your divine Higher Self that you are not paying attention, that you are not ready to learn, and asking for the pattern to repeat. On an energy level you are creating a mismatch between the energy signature of the messages being sent out by your physical mind and body, and that of your divine truth.

Throughout the rest of this book I will show you how to align these so that negativity, pain and suffering completely disappear from your life in its entirety.

The more you embrace you and what is going on inside and its impact on your life, the better your life will become. If this makes you feel excited – great! If it makes you feel nervous – take note: your Ego wants your attention. If it fills you with dread or fear, what you resist will persist until you embrace it. Again, take note.

As you may have realized from **Exercise 1** above, "Who are you being when you are being you", negativity can be a small part, a large part or even consume your life. It is part of you; it is part of your life experience and make up as a human being... but, you were just meant to take note, learn and release the energy. Unfortunately for some they made the void bigger by living there! It is now time to change that.

18

There are patterns to your negativity. That is why the same thing keeps happening! It has meaning! There is something for you to notice. There is something fundamental that you need to learn that will help you in your life, to heal some aspect of your life you are not happy with. The combination of your self-talk, thoughts, feelings, actions, behaviors and emotional wellbeing in given situations highlights a key that will help you to understand and decipher their meaning. *This is called the Ego's Code.*

For you to start to understand your negativity, why it happens, when it happens, the form it takes, its size, its scale and its meaning, you need to embrace it and own it.

It is time to go into the resistance...

The Gift of My Negativity

This is a very simple and straightforward exercise. It is also a very cathartic and often liberating exercise. In the space below, simply express and write down the negativity you experience in your life. If you don't want to write it below because someone else may see it, honor your feelings and use a private journal.

EXERCISE 2

If you are struggling to express your negativity 'in general,' think of a situation or circumstance where you experienced a negative reaction (whether publically or privately) and note how it made you feel. What thoughts went through your head? What did you say to yourself? How did you treat yourself? How did you treat anyone else involved? What behaviors showed up? Did you feel off balance, out of sync, emotionally weak? What happened...?

EXERCISE 2

Please Note: *When you do this exercise do not relive the situation... just express yourself! If you still struggle, close your eyes, take a deep breath, put your hand on your heart, and tell yourself you are OK and that you are safe. Then just write. After you have finished, get yourself a glass of water, go outside and breathe in some fresh air. Later I will share with you why it often feels soooooo good to do this!*

In the space below, simply express and write down the negativity you experience in your life.

_____

_____

_____

_____

_____

_____

_____

_____

_____

_____

You Matter!

THE LAST chapter gave you a little more awareness about the purpose of negativity and your Ego's role in your life. Exercise 2 also helped you to understand some of the negativity you experience day-to-day. Both exercises completed so far offer some useful insight that you can use later when I explain how to decipher your Ego's Code, but at this early stage it is possible for both exercises to be intellectualized, keeping you at an arm's length from you. Let me explain...

As I explored my Ego's code and made changes to my life, one of the most consistent messages that kept coming up for me was how 'I' felt, about 'me'. In the previous chapter, I shared that one of my core life lessons is about receiving love. I thought this was solely about being able to receive love from others, but to my surprise this also included love 'from me', 'to me'. This was *not* something I found very easy, and in fact something I realized I avoided at all cost. My avoidance to receive love showed up in many ways e.g., I would avoid spending time with me by procrastinating and escaping my life by watching television; I would reject and deflect compliments from others or say someone else deserved it; I would come up with excuses to avoid social situations where I would have to share me and then I would beat myself up for not going. One of the most consistent consequences of not allowing myself to receive love was with my weight. My weight would regularly fluctuate up and down. On one occasion, I weighed 252 pounds. I remember on several occasions, I would literally "stuff" my face with chocolate... often 10 or more bars a day. Packets of cookies were also another favorite. When I explored this further, I realized that I did not matter to me and that I did not want to matter to others.

Despite the image I shared with the outside world, one of togetherness, strength, determination, drive, ambition, caring and understanding, inside I was feeling uncertain, nervous, anxious, fearful, resentful and angry. I was regularly putting others ahead of me. In the majority of situations, I would put myself second, or third, or last. One day I paused and actually heard myself saying quietly to myself "You don't matter", "You are insignificant", "You cannot be loved" – guess how that showed up in my health, in my relationships, in my business, and in my relationship with money?

In deciphering my code and making the changes I wanted for me in my life I needed to raise my awareness of the unconscious stories I regularly told myself, the stories that caused me to get in my own way. With this new awareness, I consciously refocused myself to move forward in the way I chose.

The "You don't matter" story you tell yourself can show up in more than one way. It has many forms and wears many masks. In this chapter I am going to share with you examples of the stories I have told myself, the masks I have worn in my own life and seen on others I have worked with, together with a mantra from your Ego's Code which when you use it every day will help you reduce the impact and effects of the stories you tell yourself. In a later chapter, when we look deeper at how you decipher your code, I will share with you more detailed steps you can use to counteract and change your story so that you can fully embrace you and design the life you want to live.

> *What is a mantra?* *Mantras are a tool used to move you from a place of scattered thought and outward focus, to focused thought and inner focus. These mantras will act as an effective tool to help you focus, calm, and train your mind so that you can start to free yourself from the stories you tell yourself and the masks you wear.*

The stories fall into the 8 categories below.

STORY 1 – *I should keep quiet*

STORY 2 – *I can't think for myself*

STORY 3 – *I don't feel*

STORY 4 – *I can't be me*

STORY 5 – *I am unlovable*

STORY 6 – *I don't get involved*

STORY 7 – *I don't like me.*

STORY 8 – *It's safer to play small*

The reason you experience a story is because unconsciously you still feel unsafe e.g., unsafe to voice your opinions, unsafe to think for yourself, unsafe being successful and so on. As for negativity, *ALL* stories, without exception, relate to your past, whether that is the past in your current lifetime or from your past lives. You may experience one, more than one, or many stories in your life. But you will experience at least one. Each story has arisen from any one or a combination of the traumas you have experienced in your past. Or a story may have arisen because in the past, you were given a lot of attention or recognition for behavior linked to a story.

Rationally, when you consciously reflect on each story, they may or may not make sense unless you are aware of them or notice the pattern.

Spiritually, they make perfect sense! They form part of the divine spiritual system and there is a divine order to them.

In service to you, your Ego has invited you into repetitive situations for you to learn from your story or stories, to heal or to become whole. But here's your challenge - your human fight, flight or freeze response has been conditioned to do all that you can to avoid the situation... until now.

The voices in your head

Each story begins with an unconscious thought, which is often accompanied by a voice in your head (which can be as quiet as a whisper, but it is there). My question to you is this, when you hear the little voice in your head, do you hear you? Is there one voice or more than one? This may seem strange, but you may hear someone else's voice, a parent, grandparent, a friend, a teacher, or a boss. It may be the phrase, their tone, the energy or even the sound of the voice that will let you know. You are not crazy or going crazy! In fact this is normal.

Illustration 3 - *The Voices in Your Head*

What is abnormal is whether or not it serves you at the highest level. For example, sometimes I just like to relax in front of the TV and eat my dinner. But when I am preparing my food I regularly hear the commanding words of my Dad, with his finger pointing at me saying, *"TRAY! TRAY! I don't want you spilling any food on our carpets. When you have your own house you can do what you like, but as long as you live here, you will use a tray!"* In the past, when I "tried" not using a tray I experienced anxiety and worry about making a mess. On a spiritual level I also experienced the energy associated with my dad's command. What is interesting is how something that appears so small can have such a huge impact on my life and has done for years. Whilst my dad was seeking to teach me about standards and respect, the stories I have told myself from this one repetitive event include it's safer to keep quiet, don't share what I am thinking or feeling, it is unsafe to be me because if I do, I will get shouted at! A number of these stories have shown up so many times and in so many different ways in my life. Once I understand the pattern and recognize that it is not my voice or my energy I can then choose what to learn and keep from this interaction (e.g. high standards and self-respect are a good thing) and what to let go because it does not serve me (e.g. not being able to express my thoughts or feelings about it). Then I can live my life for me.

Later you will understand how other people have impacted upon how you see, feel and experience the world. All of which are gifts. Some will impact on how you behave and show up in life. Through reading this book you will have a choice about what you want to keep for you and what you want to get rid of because it does not serve you. For now, I am going to share with you the essentials you need to start raising your awareness.

STORY 1 – *I should keep quiet*

The mantra from your Ego's Code is
my voice matters; I love my voice!

You have a voice for very important reasons, namely to share your thoughts, feelings, opinions, insights, and wisdom, but if you have experienced anything like the following e.g. continually being ignored, talked over, shouted at, put down or punished for being outspoken (in this life or a past life), you may shy away from sharing or even hide (physically or inside), what is real and true for you. Remember, the core reason for all the "stories" you tell yourself is to keep you safe and avoid being hurt again as you were in the past – and that is a good thing , but it stops you from fully experiencing the best of you and your life. As a result you may feel your opinion is not important, or that you want to avoid hurting someone else, or you just want to fit in and be liked. For me, it was all about avoiding conflict. The thought in my head was "it is safer to keep the peace." My behavior reflected this through silence, withdrawal, deflection or even lies. My favorite phrases included, "Oh, don't ask me" or "What's the point? I'll only be disappointed again" or "I don't want to disappoint you." The reasons will be different for different people.

Within my corporate work I regularly come across this in organizations, departments and teams where there is a fear culture. The fear has often been caused through "fear of repercussion." Consistently I hear the people in the teams say *"I could never say that to him or her because..."* The 'because' is always to do with self-preservation to avoid the perceived pain of consequence either for themselves or the other person. This is one of the major reasons a culture never changes, often perpetuates and spirals downwards.

In one organization I worked with, the Sales Director who was a driven, focused and highly assertive woman had created a 'fear' culture. She had a sales team of 10 sales staff, all of whom were terrified of her to such an extent that they collectively agreed to lie to her about the number of client calls they were making, the number of meetings they were attending and the number of sales in the pipeline. In several discussions about her poor leadership behavior and the poor behavior of her team she completely denied it was happening – she did not see it or didn't want to see it. I offered different solutions including one to one coaching, team building that focused on creating openness and trust and anonymous 360 feedback, all of which would have given everyone the opportunity to share what was going on for them personally and help resolve the low morale and under performance. But, she replied, "I don't care what they have to say. All I care about is them delivering results..." But the results were false. She did not care about, let alone want to hear their voices. In my experience a person or company will only change if they want to change. If they don't want to change or grow, there is no point in wasting time, energy or money. In fewer than 12 months this company was no longer in existence. It's a real shame because the company had a great reputation for delivering fantastic results to their clients, but there was a massive incongruence to how they showed up for their clients and how they showed up in their own work environment. Furthermore, in life or in business when there is a rotten apple in a key position of influence, who does not care about what people have to say, the rot can spread and eventually destroy or infect someone or something that is great.

There is a spiritual paradox here to highlight. If you consider that your ego will guide you to situations and environments where you can learn and heal, if you find yourself in a situation in your personal or work life where you are experiencing fear of expressing your voice, take note - you are there for a reason!

It is your birthright and your divine right to be heard. You have a right to share what you need to be happy. If someone or a group of people are undermining your point of view in any way, you have a decision to make for you.

Reflect on a time in your past when you did express your voice with passion and energy. Remember what it felt like.

What happened to give you the courage to speak up? Ask yourself how did you find the energy to make this change? What was going on for you at that time, because if you can find that energy once, you can find it again!

Power Animal – *The Blue Whale*
The blue whale is the loudest mammal on earth.
Blue whales mostly emit very loud, highly structured, repetitive low-frequency rumbling sounds that can travel for many miles underwater.

Call upon and work with the Blue Whale,
if you need help with:
Expressing your voice
Finding your voice
Finding the song in your heart

STORY 2 – *I can't think for myself*

The mantra from your Ego's Code is
my thoughts matter; I easily think for myself!

I learned many years ago, that when I say 'yes' to something or someone in my life then I am saying 'no' to something or someone else. For example, writing this book took a lot of time, energy and focused attention. Saying 'yes' to writing meant that I said 'no' on many occasions to spending time with my family. In my learning about the Ego's Code I have found that this story often partners Story 1 - 'I must keep quiet' for similar reasons to those we discussed above. However, I would go one step further and say that this story can have a deeper and more painful impact on the way you experience life because as a minimum it can cause you to appear detached and become isolated, or at an extreme, completely incapacitated.

This story takes you outside of yourself and keeps you outside of yourself because you could see everyone as being better than you, having better thoughts or ideas than you, that you're not good enough, no matter how hard you try. People with this story can struggle to make decisions, can't or won't make decisions or they question the decisions they do make so much so that they backtrack, stay still or keep themselves hidden.

More often than not, decisions are made by reaching out to others for 'advice' with the advice given being taken as the answer whether or not it feels right, serves you or not. Then the other person or people become a crutch or constant source of solution and you become reliant upon them. Depending on who that person is and how much they love to 'give advice' or 'be in control' can keep you trapped outside of yourself. This Story can be so significant that it can render you incapable of looking after yourself. At an extreme, the most basic life decisions become difficult from what to eat, what to wear, where to shop and so on.

When questioned by an authority figure you may feel bombarded and experience what I would call a 'brain freeze' meaning you just can't think of an answer. Your internal voice may appear childlike and say, 'just sit and behave then everything will be okay.'

Your thoughts are so important and have such an important meaning. If you disregard your thoughts, you disregard you.

Your thoughts flow from the essence of who you are at a soul level. So, if your thoughts shape your experiences, shape your personality and shape the reality of the life you experience every day, then to disregard and deny your thoughts, is a denial of your very soul. Thoughts are things! If you want to change your life then you need to own your thoughts.

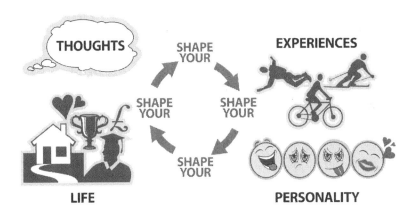

THOUGHTS   SHAPE YOUR   EXPERIENCES

SHAPE YOUR   SHAPE YOUR

SHAPE YOUR

LIFE   PERSONALITY

Illustration 4 - Thoughts are Things

STORY 3 – *I don't feel*

⸭ **The mantra from your Ego's Code is**
⸭ *my feelings matter; I can show or share*
⸭ *my feelings if I choose to!*

I used to tell myself the story that I don't feel, but the real story was that I don't **show** my feelings or in some cases the story I don't **share** my feelings.

The easy way to check that you have a pulse and feel is the Sex Test! Remember the last orgasm you had. Provided you didn't fake it, I know you felt something!

Feelings are fundamental in helping you to fully experience all your life has to offer. As you know some feel good and positive, others feel bad and negative. The interesting and important thing to understand is that neither is more important than the other. Your feelings are your feelings. They are real! They are ALL important and they ALL matter because they are messages from you to you. It's what you do with them that matters. I have no intention of telling you how you should feel and neither should anyone else. However, I am going to distinguish between positive and negative feelings because it will help you to understand what is real and right for you and where you can learn to help you experience more consistent joy in your life. Positive feelings include (but are not limited to) happiness, awe, excitement, joy and bliss. Negative feelings include (but are not limited to) anger, sadness, fear, shame and guilt.

Your feelings are a sensory trigger that generates a chemical response in your body to either an external or internal event to help you make meaning of what is going on around you and inside you. An external event can be any situation, experience or interaction. An internal event can be a thought or something you say to yourself. The response is a message to you, from you, and can have a number of meanings. At its most basic level, the message will be "this feels bad" or "this feels good."

With all feelings, the response tends to have a short, medium or long duration; it can be on the surface or deep in the body; it can be located in a certain part of the body and it has a degree of intensity from a murmur to an elevated spike e.g. experiencing happiness with a rush of dopamine and you feel awesome. Then after a while the intensity begins to level out and the feeling reduces. The same happens when you experience sadness and stress, there is intensity, combined with cortisol, and you feel bad. But again, after a while the intensity begins to level out and fade away. Interestingly though, have you ever noticed that unconsciously we tend to hang on to negative feelings for longer? How amazing would it be if we could reverse engineer this and consciously experience our joy for longer periods of time? In fact, why not all the time?!

What is dopamine? *Dopamine is a neurotransmitter in the brain that helps control the reward and pleasure centers, i.e. when it is released it makes you feel good.*

What is cortisol? *Cortisol is essential to the human brain's functioning. It is produced by the adrenal glands and help cells create energy from food. When your body experiences stress, whether physical, mental, or emotional, more cortisol is created by the adrenals in order to protect the body. This charge of cortisol is part of what's known as the "fight or flight" response, which occurs when your body prepares itself to handle a stressful event. This response is key to your ability to act quickly in an emergency.*

So how do you respond to your feelings?
Do you acknowledge them and feel them?
Do you feel some and not others?
Do you ignore them and push them down?
Do you tell yourself a story? If so, which one?

It is crucial in life to acknowledge your feelings, because without them you are merely existing rather than fully experiencing and expressing the best of you, and the best of your life. On a personal note, over the years this has been something I have found very hard to do, but worse still I thought that I did not feel because I often felt empty or numb. As a result, for so many years I suffocated myself in my life. It was like I could not breathe but I did not know why. Below is an example of a story I used to tell myself. It's called, 'Why don't we celebrate?'

In all areas of my life I have experienced success that I should have celebrated but in the past I never did. For example, regularly, we would win a big deal in our company, which by all accounts should have been celebrated to the max but in one breath and in one swift movement (without even a pause for thought) I would move straight on to the next thing, and then on to the next thing, and on to the next thing.

After a while my wife and partner in our business would ask, "Why are we not celebrating?" I had no response. I was dumbstruck. There was literally nothing inside me.

On a reflection, there were a few things going on here. First of all when we won our deals the feeling of the win was neutral, I did not 'feel' anything, let alone the need to celebrate... which was a problem I had not noticed. For me it was all the action before the deal was concluded that was the "juice." Understanding our clients' needs, the negotiation, building the solution, and later, ultimately the delivery. However, as you know, one of my lessons in life is about receiving and *feeling* love from others. This was yet another example of me not wanting to receive the feeling of love from my girls who wanted to acknowledge our success and me. But there is a second lesson for me to share with you. It's not just what you feel that is important, it is what you are not feeling that is equally important to notice.

The second thing going on here was that I was overlooking my girls' desire to celebrate, which meant that I was ignoring their feelings, which is also a problem and something in life we need to be aware of and own.

The third thing is that I was showing no appreciation or gratitude for the work we had won.

In today's modern world, society expects everything at speed, which is absolutely okay, provided we give ourselves the gift of space to pause, to feel, to appreciate and to express gratitude. Otherwise we can lose sight of who we are and then start to live life upside down and out of flow.

The above was so enlightening for me that I needed to unpack this further. The first thing that I did was spend some time seeking to understand why I did not want to celebrate. I realized this came from my parents. I remember being told when I passed exams, and wanting a reward for my success, that the reward for passing exams is the reward itself. It was at this point I decided to make a change. I realized that the child inside me took my parents literally. I took charge and updated my internal messages by giving myself permission to celebrate and to acknowledge my successes by rewarding myself with a meaningful gift that represented in mind the size of the success e.g. from a massage, to dinner at a nice restaurant, to a Mont Blanc pen.

For my girls, we have a social agreement in our home about inclusion and that all feelings matter. To express our feelings safely, we need to feel safe otherwise we will deflect or avoid. We pause, we listen and ensure each person is heard and then decide together how we are going to celebrate together. Finally, we always show appreciation and express gratitude for our clients.

If you are someone who does not like to show your feelings, do not make this a bad thing. On some level it has served you in the past by keeping you safe. My invitation to you is to notice what is going on for you and to acknowledge your feelings. Then, when you are ready, you choose for you, when you want to make a change, if you want to make a change and what change is right for you.

STORY 4 – *I can't be me*

The mantra from your Ego's Code is
I am always me; it is safe to be me!

99% of people who I give psychic readings to are in search of an answer to the question - What is my purpose? Your purpose is to be you! Therefore, there is an obvious paradox, because every soul has something to learn. As a result, there is always a natural distance between whom you project out in the world today and you. (See illustration on page 37).

Your purpose through being you is to close this gap! The more you learn from your negativity, the more of your Ego you release, the more you Expand your Greatness Out and experience you.

The challenge is that as a human being, we can become consumed by the negativity and become victims of what we perceive to be our own reality. As a result, we don't learn, we continue to create the same old shit in our life and the spiral continues downwards, sometimes out of control.

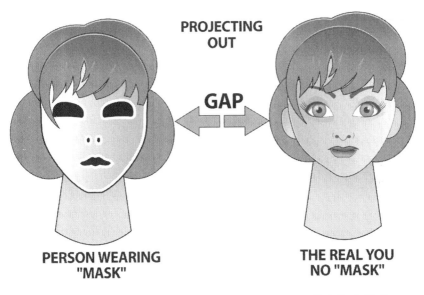

Illustration 5 - *The Gap*

What if where you are right now is where you are meant to be, as crazy as that sounds or as much as you hate the idea of that? And what if the person you are being right now is the person you are meant to be at this stage in your life? If that were true, it gives you permission to take the pressure off. It does not mean stop and settle. It enables you to be present with yourself, to notice you, to see you in all your glory, with all your faults, with all your quirks and magnificence. From this place of grounded peace, you can see the next steps you need to take to evolve. This can be as rapid or as steady as you choose for you. Whatever feels right! You just need to take them.

As you learn and Expand your Greatness Out, you will see that your reality will change with you because you are changing. We will talk more about this in the next chapter.

If you have the Story 'I can't be me', be clear about what you mean. Do you mean you have a yearning to be more of who you are in your heart and soul or do you mean that you can't express the essence of who you are today because of the environment, or circumstances you find yourself in?

In both cases, there is something for you to learn about honoring you, respecting you and seeing you for who you are. When you combine all three you will feel the courage, drive and power to fully embrace you.

The important point to note here is that there could be a scale to the intensity. If it is simply the environment e.g. a workplace where you just don't fit and you know it, you have control to change it to an environment where you can express and experiment with you. If it is a controlling relationship, then you may need help to understand what you need and help finding the courage to be you again.

No matter what the environment or circumstance, do not settle, because to settle means you are denying your true purpose.

STORY 5 – *I am unlovable*

The mantra from your Ego's Code is
I am worthy of love; I openly receive love into all aspects of my life.

When I reflect on my life, I have never been surrounded by a lot of close friends. In fact, I have always been very selective about the people I hang out with. I kept most people at an arm's length so that I did not have to get close to them or let them get close to me. Unconsciously, I would put such high expectations and impossible demands on people that they would never be able to meet; then they would disappoint me, let me down and I would leave or I would sabotage the relationship so they would leave me. This would confirm the Story I would tell myself - that *I am unlovable*.

I also mastered the art of deflection by only sharing the parts of me that scratched the surface, or avoiding the opportunity to connect with someone fully by engulfing and dominating the situation making it all about the other person, so I did not have to share or receive attention and recognition, whether that be love, kindness, or even help.

I remember as a thirteen year old boy, and I say boy consciously, that a close girl friend gave me a hug. It was the first *real* hug that I can remember. When I say *real* hug, I don't mean what I would call a 'man hug' when two guys come together and pat each other's back and move away quickly. I mean a real hug – a hug when someone literally holds you close, holds you tight, comforts you, for more than five breaths. I recall experiencing a tear and what felt like joyful fear. I also remember saying out loud "Wow! What was that?" and being told that was a hug. The joy was wonderful, but I do recognize there was fear of being close and wanting to run.

The Story I am unlovable, can also be flipped on its head. I have been known *not* to let people get close to me, because I feared letting them down and causing them pain. Guess what, this is exactly what I did. I was a master of the self-fulfilling prophecy. We will be talking about this at length in a later chapter.

Don't get me wrong, I do have a very close, but also small inner circle of people I love very much and I know love me; a group of friends I have built up over time, who I feel safe sharing my vulnerability with, a group of people who will not judge me, but do call me out when my *shit* gets in the way. Interestingly they often see it coming before I do. The great thing is that they help me to see it, so I can learn from my Ego's Code.

But I do still recognize I am not very tolerant. Often it only takes a small situation or event and I will withdraw! Often they won't even know it has happened, let alone why. This is something that I am still learning to let go and still seeking to master. Some things take a little more time, effort and focus.

Often at the center of this Story is trust. If you tell yourself this story, are you someone who gives 100% of your trust completely unconditionally, often without basis, or are you often wary of people and hold it back until there is proof that they are trustworthy? My guess is that in both situations, you find people often let you down or you sabotage the relationship confirming your Story that you are unlovable because people leave you.

The very important point to note is that just because someone tells themselves this Story does not mean they have poor social skills, or cannot build relationships or get close to people. I have awesome social skills, and I build rapport and relationships very easily, but the majority of my relationships have been very 'business like', because of an unconscious fear of letting people in because *people leave* and *I could get hurt.* When I experience this today, I recognize that I am reliving a past experience both from this life time as a child, and also from many of my past lives because this Story can leave me feeling very raw.

I am sharing examples from my life so that you can see examples of the behavior that may show up in your life. If you tell yourself this Story, you may recognize some or all of the above. I know from personal experience, that telling yourself this Story can be very lonely and lead to a superficial existence, which is why I invite you to choose your life partner and peer group wisely. Sharing my life with Lindsay has transformed the way I look at and experience relationships. I have learned to truly share me and it is a wonderful experience when someone touches your heart and allows you to touch theirs. It is the same with my friendships. I invite you to take the risk, share you, all of you and see what happens. It is truly magical.

STORY 6 – *I don't get involved*

The mantra from your Ego's Code is
I am free to take care of myself and others;
I always do what I say I am going to do.

Don't get involved has two Stories – I don't get involved in my own life and I certainly don't get involved in anybody else's life.

Your thoughts, feelings, emotions, and self-talk all drive your behaviors, how you act and how you show up in your life. Hence they are one of the biggest indicators about what is going on inside. Therefore, if you have trouble identifying any of the Stories you tell yourself, just look at your behavior and work backwards. What do I mean? In the past I demonstrated behavior that involved stuffing my face with food, cookies and chocolate (when I was not hungry) to the extent that I could not speak. Besides the negative by-product of putting on weight, the behavior was consistent when I had something important I should share with my family or friends. The stuffing kept me quiet, enabled me to procrastinate and avoid speaking up i.e. it supported my Story "I must keep quiet."

Your behavior is also the biggest indicator of your integrity and how genuine you are. Do you do what you say you are going to do - for others AND for you?

So many times I see business leaders say one thing and their actions demonstrate that they are not aligned to it and do something completely different. Take ethics as an example. Society today expects businesses and their leaders to do the right thing. So many organizations have a corporate code of conduct that says they will behave in a certain way, but until they are living and breathing it in every action, every transaction and in every behavior, it is just "another initiative." The tone from the top in organizations (i.e. the behavior shown by the Board of Directors) is always a key indicator of whether the values of an organization are being upheld and lived by. Then there is the question, does the tone from the top flow through the middle to the teams on the ground, or is it getting stuck in the middle because there is no buy-in?

So how does this relate to you in your life?

Do your behaviors represent who you say you are? Are they representative of who you are in your heart and soul? Or are they a projection of the image you portray to the outside world but are the opposite of who you really are? Do you regularly get in your own way and sabotage your success? I invite you to pause and reflect on these questions before moving on.

Finally, what do you do if you see behaviors that are inappropriate or just downright wrong? Do you stop and call out the situation and person or do you walk past it? If you walk past you are indirectly making that person's behavior okay. Do you own your behavior or do you just walk on by?

Consider the following true story.

My niece broke her coccyx (tailbone). Six months into her healing she was on crutches travelling by bus to see a friend. When she arrived at her destination, she was supposed to have disability support from the bus company, but no one showed up. My niece took it upon herself to see if she could manage with her bags all the way to the Arrivals Desk. Unfortunately, she fell over in the road, her bags sprawled everywhere. She really hurt herself. Despite her tears, despite her bags being in the road, despite her being in a dangerous situation, not one person (and I mean no one) stopped to help her. EVERYONE just walked past her.

What would you do? Do you also have a Story that says, "Don't get involved"?

Pause for a moment and honestly reflect on how you would act. If you would walk past, at the core of your decision is that you don't feel that you matter, and the person in pain is being a gift to you by acting as a reflection of yourself, because in that moment you don't think they matter either.

My question to you is what would have to happen for you to take action, to step up?

When we examine our behaviors, we will have good, strong, positive behaviors that are aligned to who we are in our truth and we will have behaviors that cause us to get in our own way that can directly or indirectly put us in harm's way, but it is important to acknowledge that any non-action is also a choice to behave in a certain way.

When something is not working for you in your life and you are experiencing negativity, you are misaligned, lacking integrity with yourself and it will show up in your behaviors. Below is a quick exercise called *Mismatch* which I learned from working with a group of teenagers in Denmark many years ago that I found very illuminating and now use regularly in my own life, with my personal clients and my corporate clients.

EXERCISE 3

Mismatch

Equipment: You will need a piece of paper and a pen.

First of all here is a worked example: Place both of your hands out in front of you palms facing up.

In your left hand, is something that is important to you in your life, for example, your health.

In your right hand, are the actions and behaviors that you need to demonstrate on a daily basis to honor your health, for example, taking regular exercise, drinking plenty of water, eating healthy foods, meditation, relaxation, sleep, etc.

When your actions and behaviors are aligned as in this example to your health, you can put your hands together... and applaud yourself, because you are being congruent! You are doing what you say you will do.

If your actions and behaviors are not aligned with what is important to you for health, your hands do not come together, in fact they cross over and miss each other. There is no applause... instead there is frustration, anxiety, sadness and probably weight gain.

Now, consider the areas in your life that are important to you, but are not working. Repeat this exercise as many times as you need. Notice your behaviors and where there is alignment and more importantly where there is a misalignment. Then decide for you what actions you are going to take to change them.

STORY 7 - *I don't like me*

The mantra from your Ego's Code is
I am always kind to me; it is safe to love me.

The second you judge someone; you lose all ability to influence them.

The second you judge yourself; you lose all ability to influence and impact your life.

The first line of this quote was shared with me on a course I attended years ago that stuck with me. The second line is what I call a *Claytonism* and one I regularly use in my life when I think about how I see myself, and when making decisions in my life. I invite you to do the same, especially as we continue through this chapter.

"I see you" were three words I said to my wife long before they were said in the famous film *Avatar*. When I look at her,

I see beyond her external beauty, I see her magnificence, her grace, her finesse, her majesty and her true divine essence that radiates out of her and connects with all things. I see and feel the impact she has on me, our daughter, her friends, and our clients and I know that from any and all interactions, however brief, she has made their lives better in some way. So I know she matters.

When I look at the world today I see so many incredible people, making the world a better place. So I know that they matter.

Every person, *every* soul on our wonderful planet has an important purpose, an important story to share. Even if it helps just one person, they matter, because it's the ripple effects of their contribution... and it's for that reason I know you matter.

But it is all well and good me saying that if you don't know that for yourself or you tell yourself the Story that you don't like yourself... *yet*!

You have a story, a story that matters, a story that can make a difference, for you and for others. Whether your story is one of happiness and joy, or one of hardship, trauma and devastation. It matters because good or bad it has meaning for you. A meaning that will help you to live the story you choose, for you - the one you design.

But how your story unfolds and whether you live a rich life or merely exist will be determined by how you see, think and feel about you consciously and unconsciously plus how you behave towards you, towards others and the things you say to yourself in private.

Jim Rohn once said, *"If you don't design your own life plan, chances are you'll fall into someone else's plan. And guess what they have planned for you? Not much."*

My interpretation of this insightful message is that "if *you* don't make a choice, then someone will make a choice for you" and ten times out of ten, it will be the wrong choice, because only you truly know you what is right for you.

So let's find out what you see...

What Do I See?

This is a three-stage exercise, for which you will need a full-length mirror, paper and a pen.

*STAGE 1 – **Simply go and look at yourself in the mirror.***

Make a note on the paper the thoughts that come up, how you are feeling, what you say to yourself, and anything you notice about you.

STAGE 2 – "I love you"

This time when you look at yourself in the mirror, look into your eyes, truly see you and say to yourself, "I love you."

Again, make a note on the paper what you are feeling, how comfortable or uncomfortable you are, what you say to yourself positive and negative, any and all thoughts that come up.

Stage 3 – "In private"

This time, I invite you to stand in front of your mirror naked for just 2 minutes.

Again, make a note on the paper how you are feeling, how comfortable you are and specifically what you say to yourself positive and negative, any and all thoughts that come up.

EXERCISE 4

Option for Stage 3 – When you are naked standing in front of the mirror, pause, breathe in and say to yourself, "I love you." Notice is this easy or hard? Again, make a note about how you are feeling, how comfortable you are and specifically what you say to yourself, any and all thoughts that come up.

All the exercises in Part 1 of this book are about "awareness." The more awareness you have about you in your life, the more understanding you will have, the better the conscious choices you will make for you. But, unlike the first two exercises, this exercise will generate an emotional response and starts to identify some of the Stories you tell yourself in your life.

So with this in mind, I invite you to notice whether you:

- **Completed all three stages?**
- **Completed some stages and not others?**
- **Pretended to do them?**
- **Skipped them altogether, promising yourself you would do them later, but really knowing you will never do them?**

Whatever you chose to do, it is important for you to notice what is going on inside and start to notice when similar thoughts, feelings, emotions, behaviors, actions, and self-talk show up elsewhere in your life.

So, what did you notice?

What were your thoughts - Is anyone looking at me? Am I really going to do this? Can I do this? This is going to be difficult? This is stupid? I feel silly?

What were your feelings? Anxiety? Nervousness? Resistance? Pressure? Excitement? Happiness? Wonder?

What things did you say to yourself? "I can't look at you!", "Wow! You are hot!", "You've put on a few pounds!", "You're too fat!", "You're too thin!", "I don't need to do this!" "I love you!"

What actions or behaviors did you take or want to take? To run? To escape? To look deeper? To look closer? To admire? To smile?

Whatever you thought, felt, said to yourself or how you behaved toward yourself is perfect. Just be aware of it and do not make yourself wrong! The most important thing is to be honest with you, be real, because it has meaning.

If you avoided the exercise, notice are you giving yourself a *true* reason (i.e. the truth) or a *false* excuse (i.e. a lie) to sidestep getting to know you. From my own life experience when you lie to yourself, there is an unconscious decision being made that "you don't matter to you."

Ask yourself the question, "why am I stopping myself from having a relationship with myself?"

The worst thing you could do is pretend that everything is okay, put your mask back on, and plod on with your life, living in the past.

Consider the following poem by **Dale Wimbrow**, *(1895-1954)*

When you get what you want in your struggle for pelf,
And the world makes you king for a day,
Then go to the mirror and look at yourself,
And see what the guy has to say.

For it isn't your Father, Mother or Wife,
Whose judgment upon you must pass.
The feller whose verdict counts most in your life,
Is the guy staring back from the glass.

He's the feller to please, never mind all the rest,
For he's with you clear up to the end,
And you've passed your most dangerous, difficult test,
If the guy in the glass is your friend.

You may be like Jack Horner and 'chisel' a plum,
And think you're a wonderful guy,
But the man in the glass says you're only a bum
If you can't look him straight in the eye.

You can fool the whole world down the pathway of years,
And get pats on the back as you pass,
But your final reward will be heartaches and tears,
If you've cheated the guy in the glass

The last thing I would ever want for you is to cheat the person looking back at you in your glass, because then we all lose!

So let's explore and debrief the exercise.

Most people feel very comfortable with Stage 1. They will quite happily look in the mirror at themselves. Often this is because it forms part of our daily routine to do so, e.g. when we brush our hair or wash our face in the morning. It is automatic, but it is also intellectual. We can do this without any real connection or intimacy with ourselves. The little voice in your head is there, but often goes unnoticed. But the impact it has is to reinforce old patterns.

Now, Stage 2 makes the exercise more intimate. It requires you to truly see you, to connect with you and then saying 'I love you' takes it up a notch. Most people find this uncomfortable and actually avoid the exercise or pretend to do it by not looking in their eyes. In fact, their eyes drift to look over their shoulder or down at the floor. This is also when the little voice in their head starts to become quite vocal and you start to take notice. Whatever happened for you in the exercise, just be honest with yourself. If you felt uncomfortable say so, if you felt okay, that's great. There is no right or wrong answer.

Stage 3 is often the most difficult for people. To see yourself naked in the mirror is a playground for your ego. Did you start to see what you perceive to be flaws? When I did this exercise I found myself saying "Oooh, Clayton, you could do with losing a few pounds" "Oooh, that's a bit of a Santa Belly." The first time I did this exercise I could not say "I love you" because I blamed myself for the problems in my life. Now it's easy. As you start to get to know you even better, by completing the exercises in this book, it will become easier for you too.

STORY 8 – *It is safer to play small*

The mantra from your Ego's Code is
I am successful in all areas of my life.

Before we explore this Story, pause for a moment and ask yourself, what success means to you because with all the Stories we tell ourselves, they have a personal meaning for you and show up in your life in a way only you will understand them. All I can do is to open the door to awareness and give you some things to think about.

On a recent event, when I asked some of the participants what success meant to them, the words that consistently came up were fame and fortune, materialism, money, being well known, being in the limelight or being a successful author, speaker, accountant, business man, etc. The most consistent association was money!

This is also something that regularly comes up for people in my readings with personal coaching clients and with corporate clients in particular, How can I win more clients? Because more clients means more sales, which means more money = success!

So if I use money as an example you can then map across the same approach to other areas you want to be successful in. In my own experience I have found that this Story operates on a continuum of stages where you can move from Poverty to Wealth to Riches or if you choose, straight to Riches... it's up to you!

Pause and consider 'what is your relationship with money' (or being successful at... 'X')?

What do you associate with money?

When you think about money what thoughts come up for you?

What feelings do you experience in your body?

How and where do your feelings impact your body?

What do you say to yourself about money?

**How do you act and behave when
your bills come in?**

**Are you living payday to payday?
Or pay check to pay check?**

**What do you think about people who
have more money that you?**

**What do you think about people who
are more successful than you?**

When I reflect on my past, I always had challenges with money (or being truly successful). However, I have always had *just* enough, or *just* got by. And when I had money in my bank account I didn't stop and do the responsible thing like put money aside for bills, I would spend it like I was a rich man regardless of what bills I had coming in. This was the same pattern or Story I ran for years.

When I reflect back on my childhood, I remember being told many, many times 'Money does not grow on trees.' I also remember hiding away when bills had to be paid, but I never went without. I had skiing holidays, electronic games, the latest sneakers, or gadget... Do you see the pattern?

It was when I started to explore my relationship with money that I realized the Story I told myself and the pattern and the feelings inside that showed; which meant I was able to do something about it ahead of time, rather than wait for the disaster to hit so I could learn from my Ego's Code. Here's what I discovered when I paused to notice me and my relationship with money (success) ...

- My thoughts and self-talk moved towards a lack rather than abundance mindset.

- I would start to worry about being able to pay bills.

- Household appliances would start to break down around me e.g., the dishwasher would stop working, my car would leak oil, the central heating would need repairing, etc.

- I would experience a pain in my left leg, which means a fear of moving forward.

- I would experience a pain in my lower back, which is worrying about money.

- I would experience worry, anxiety, and fear.

Guess what happened? More of the same kept on happening until I chose to interrupt the pattern and decided to change my story, which I will show you how to do in the next few chapters.

As I began to take more responsibility and change my Story about money, more money came in, and because I monitored my thoughts, feelings, body, actions, behaviors, etc. I was able to notice what was happening when people offered me more money. On every single occasion when I increased my daily fees from $500 per day, to $750, to $1,250 to $1,500, to $2,250, to $2,500, to $3,000, to $5,000, I experienced similar resistance, but because I understood what was going on I was able to deal with it *ahead of time.*

Whatever success means to you, it is your birthright to experience it in all its glory and color. You are not meant to live in the past! You are only meant to learn from it, so you can experience your best life!

Why Does the Same Thing Keep Happening?

IN THE last two chapters we explored how your Ego will not only communicate with you through negativity, but also through the various masks you wear. In this chapter we are going to explore both the physical and spiritual perspective "Why we don't do better, when we know better."

Let's begin with exploring the physical perspective.

The Veil of Uncertainty

YOU are unique! From your physical appearance, the way you think and process information, the way you see, feel, hear and interpret this world, your natural strengths, talents, your fingerprints, your DNA, right down to your very soul!

EVERYTHING about you is unique to you, and because of this very special gift, the way you experience your life is unique to you. For this reason alone it is so important you live your life in a way that honors you and works for you as an individual.

The challenge is that since the day you were born, there has been so much outside influence from people who care about you e.g. family, friends, colleagues, schools, politicians, TV, magazines, celebrities, etc., telling you how you should be, how you should behave, what you should and should not think, feel and experience. So much so that today, the clarity and understanding about who you are, your purpose and what you want out of life has become clouded and in some cases lost. It's like a veil comes down over you causing your natural blueprint to become overshadowed by the beliefs of others creating a feeling of disorientation for some, through to conflict and massive uncertainty in others.

The veil is further complicated because the energy associated with the beliefs of others is taken on board as our own i.e. it transfers to us – good and bad. In the previous chapter, I shared the example of my relationship with money. When I was little I had taken on board the beliefs of my parents as my own and the energy associated with not deserving money.

Let me explain further.

Illustration 6 - *A Picture of You*

This is a picture of you when you were born. You were born with gifts, talents, strengths, wisdom etc.

Illustration 7 - *You and Your Parents*

In your life you have one or two parents (or parental figures), who have guided you through your life. Your parents, unbeknown to them, help you to learn from the traumas of your past lives imprinted in your Ego Self. As a parent myself, I always aim to guide my daughter in the best way I know how and deep down I want to be the best parent I can be, but no matter how hard I try, I know I don't always get it right. But I also know that I am fulfilling some lesson(s) for my daughter to learn.

Illustration 8 - *Your Teachers*

You then go to school and possibly university. You spend between 15 and 20 years in education. Your teachers are also there to guide you. They want to take care of you. They teach you lots of great things, help build your knowledge, including ways of being in life. They too are helping you to fulfill some lesson(s) in your life.

Illustration 9 - *Your Work Colleagues*

You leave education and you go out to work. You spend two thirds of your lifetime working, so it is important that you get this right for you. However, you make friends, you get to know colleagues, you ask for advice. All good things. Your friends and colleagues with the best intentions try to help you with your needs and challenges. And again, they are helping you to fulfill some lesson(s) in your life

Illustration 10 - *Society*

Finally, through your own interests and desires you take on board the thoughts, feelings, beliefs, and energy of society around you...

WHERE ARE YOU?

It's like you... the you that you feel inside... the you that you seek... has become lost in the crowd.

The State of Entering the Void

The uncertainty caused by the above, leads people, including you and me to go in search of what is *perceived* to be missing in life because we feel unfulfilled, i.e. what we don't have, that we believe will make us happy.

This feeling of missing something creates a mass of negative self-talk, thoughts, feelings, behaviors and emotional imbalance driven by our Egoist desires.

The important point to note is that it is not the *something* we perceive as missing that we seek (e.g. relationship, money, career), but the positive feelings and emotional wellbeing that we know in our hearts this will bring.

The consequence of this is that you then start to focus on what you don't have (i.e. what is external to you) because there is a belief that when I "have it" it will bring the joy (or some other positive feeling) you are really seeking.

Pause for a moment, and think about your life. What do you desire more than anything in the world? What do you truly want, but you don't have? What are you missing that when you have it you think your life will be complete? So, the fact that you don't have it, or maybe you already had it, but you lost it, how does that make you feel?

Here is a list of feelings that previous participants from my events shared when they did this exercise – disappointment, anger, sadness, fear that I won't ever get it or get there, worry, doubt, frustration, guilt, loss, emptiness… just to name a few.

Here is a list of things they say to themselves as a result of the above – "I'm not good enough", "I can't do it", "It will never happen", "Nothing, goes right for me", "I don't have the skills or experience", "I am not confident enough", "Everyone leaves me", "No-one listens to me"... just to name a few.

When they felt this way, how did they treat other people, like their family, friends, even a stranger in the street? Here is a list: I ignored them, I shouted at them, I did not have time for them, I resented them, I walked past – why? Because they went internal, not in a good way, so they could reflect and learn, but in a way that continued to confirm and continue the pattern.

Guess what happened then?

Yes, you are right... the negativity bred more negativity and the situations got worse and worse. The pattern repeated itself over and over again!

EXERCISE 5A

Entering the Void (PART 1)

Make a list of all the things you perceive are missing in your life – e.g. family, friends, money, home, etc.

Then write down how it makes you feel believing they are not in your life.

Okay, let's say that spiritually, negativity only accounts for 1% of your feelings and emotions. What about the 99% that is positive?

What I find interesting is that so many people do not notice or even think about the 99% of what is already great in their life. Their focus, attention and energy flow towards what is missing i.e. the 1%. If you are really honest with yourself, there will be one or two things that you are focusing on right now, the fact that they are missing from your life is causing you worry, doubt, anguish or even pain.

Where do you focus your attention?

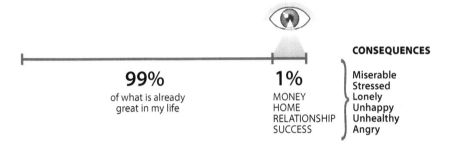

Illustration 11 - *What's Missing in Your Life?*

But, no matter what is going on in your life right now, there will be things, people, situations and experiences that are already great! It is so important that you recognize this otherwise you will continue to create the same patterns in your life that you do not want, over and over again.

The ONLY way to stop the rut is to notice what is going on inside, raise your awareness to it, learn from your Ego's Code and not get drawn into your game. Yes, you are playing a game with yourself. This is because the *Veil* created so much uncertainty that you have become lost and you've forgotten the true reasons for you being here. You have become conditioned to ignore your thoughts, feelings, emotions, behaviors, and self-talk when they are actually your route to your truth and happiness.

EXERCISE 5B

Entering the Void (PART 2)

Make a list of all the things, people, situations and experiences you already enjoy in your life that you appreciate, even if it is a list of one.

Then write down how each one makes you feel knowing that they are in your life.

If you want to create more of the great things in your life, one of the things you need to do is express gratitude and appreciation for this because just like negativity breeds negativity, gratitude and appreciation breed positivity and strength. We will talk more about this later.

So here is my question: Where are you focusing and flowing your energy and as a result, what are you creating in your life right now?

EXERCISE 6

What Am I Creating in My Life?

Here is a very straightforward exercise for you to think about where you are flowing your energy and to notice what you are creating in your life.

Put your arms by your side and lift them up until they are stretched out like you are forming a cross with your body, then turn your palms upwards.

Illustration 12 - *Where are You Focusing Your Attention?*

In your left hand is the 1% of all the negativity, pain, and/or suffering you are experiencing in your life you expressed in Exercise 5A above.

In your right hand is the 99% of great things, people, situations and experiences you identified from Exercise 5B.

Now, look at your left hand.

Here is my question. When you look at your left hand, what is going on in your right hand?

Let's debrief. When you focus on your left hand, it is not possible to see what is in your right hand. As a result, you continue to flow energy to everything that is not working or is missing in your life. Then you create more and more of the same.

However, when you focus on the 99% and live your life from here, the 1% takes care of itself!

The Biology and Science – A Brief Introduction

So many times in my readings, on my events and in corporate work, I have heard people say to me, "Well, this is the way my life has been for x number of years, I just have to put up with it! It won't change or I can't change!"

What a load of garbage!

There is a famous quote by **James Allen** *(1864-1912)* that says,

"Thoughts are things. You are today where your thoughts have brought you; you will be tomorrow where your thoughts take you"

Neuroscience has proven this is true, but before we explore what is going on inside on a cellular level, here are some facts about the brain.

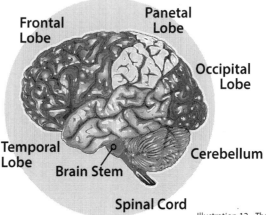

Illustration 13 - *The Brain*

The brain is one of the largest and most complex organs in your body. It is made up of more than 100 billion nerves that communicate in trillions of connections called synapses that not only put together thoughts and physical actions but also regulate your unconscious body processes, such as your digestion, pumping your heart, and your breathing.

The brain's nerve cells are known as **neurons**, which transmit and gather electrochemical signals that are communicated via a network of millions of nerve fibers called **dendrites** and **axons** as shown in illustrations 14 and 15 below.

Illustration 14 - *Dendrites and Axons*

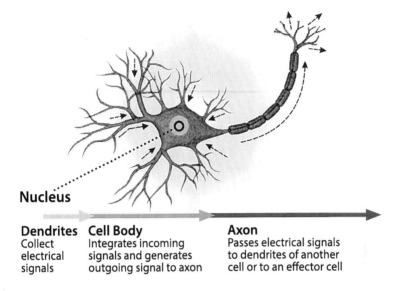

Dendrites
Collect
electrical
signals

Cell Body
Integrates incoming
signals and generates
outgoing signal to axon

Axon
Passes electrical signals
to dendrites of another
cell or to an effector cell

Illustration 15 - *Information Flow Through Neurons*

The **cerebrum** is the largest part of the brain, accounting for 85 percent of its weight.

The cerebrum has two halves, also known as hemispheres. It is further divided into four regions, or lobes, within each hemisphere. The **frontal lobes**, located behind the forehead, are focused on speech, thought, learning, emotion, and movement. Behind them are the **parietal lobes**, which process sensory information such as touch, temperature, and pain. At the rear of the brain are the **occipital lobes**, dealing with vision. Lastly, there are the **temporal lobes**, near the temples, which are involved with hearing and memory.

The second largest part of the brain is the **cerebellum**, which sits beneath the back of the **cerebrum**. It is responsible for coordinating muscle movement and controlling your balance.

The cerebellum transmits information to the spinal cord and other parts of your brain.

The **diencephalon** is located in the core of the brain. A complex of structures roughly the size of an apricot. The two major sections are the **thalamus** and **hypothalamus**. The thalamus acts as a relay station for incoming nerve impulses from around the body that are then forwarded to the appropriate brain region for processing. The hypothalamus controls hormone secretions from the nearby **pituitary gland**. These hormones govern growth and instinctual behavior such as eating, drinking, sex, anger and reproduction.

The **brain stem** controls reflexes and crucial, basic life functions such as heart rate, breathing, and blood pressure. It also regulates when you feel tired or awake.

So, what is going on at a cellular level inside your brain and inside your body that is contributing to you continuing to experience the challenges in your life? To understand this I am briefly going to explain **Hebbian Theory and Neuroplasticity.**

You would have heard at some point in your life that "practice makes perfect." But have you ever wondered why? It relates to the synaptic plasticity of your brain and the number of times a thought needs to be repeated before it becomes sufficiently hard wired into your brain.

In 1949, Canadian psychologist Donald Hebb said, "The persistence or repetition of a reverberatory activity induces lasting cellular changes that add to its stability." In other words, *"cells that fire together, wire together."*

Hebbian Learning, as it is known, explains that the simultaneous activation of cells leads to increases in synaptic strength. This is why repeated thought or practice strengthens the hardwiring of neurons in the association areas of the various lobes of your brain.

Biologically this means that a dominant thought will stimulate new synaptic connections in your brain. Once these connections are made, repetition of the same thought (or action) will stimulate more corresponding connections.

The more a thought is held (or action taken), the easier it is for that thought to be remembered or activated. For example, learning a new skill such as dancing or a new language. The more you practice, the more you improve, the more it becomes natural and instinctive.

So what about negativity? It is the same case for your negative thoughts, feelings, emotions, behaviors, memories, and self-talk.

This could be a negative story you tell yourself that you are unloved, or not good enough, or don't have the capability which, through the constant repetition over the years, is now hardwired into your survival mechanism – fight, flight or freeze. This means that this collection of thoughts is connected to the hypothalamus and pituitary and thus creates neuropeptides, which in turn encode this thought or memory at the cellular level. Therefore, any contrary thought will be resisted, as your body will have a defensive reaction to the contrary feeling.

So, how do you rid yourself of these unwanted thoughts? How can you get out of your own way?

I have often heard people talk about willpower, which is useful, but how many times have you seen someone lose weight and then put it all back on again? This is because willpower is not enough.

What about positive thinking? Again, it is not enough. How many times have you thought positively about having more money and still you don't have enough? What about love? How many times have you heard someone say, your soul mate will come to you, just be positive, but no matter how positive you are, you are still alone or you are still bouncing from relationship to relationship?

Hebbian Learning, says, "Use it or lose it." If you could select a different and more positive thought, make it as vivid as possible, and have it recurring, you will biologically rewire your brain to develop new neural pathways while weakening the unwanted negative neural networks through disuse.

When you change your thoughts, you are literally changing your brain over time. Creating a new consistent thought pattern, creates new feelings, which creates new behaviors, which creates new outcomes and hence a new life.

Meditation is a great tool for helping release resistance and to installing new thought patterns. However, repetition is still the key. Repeated meditation can be used effectively to create new neural networks in your brain, which in turn cause unwanted networks to atrophy and dissolve.

Hebbian Theory and Neuroplasticity are so important in the world today, they are even teaching this in our schools to help children at a young age understand how their brain works, and how they can improve their performance and life experiences.

So just by reading this book you are having a new experience and creating new neural pathways in your brain.

Later we will look at how to continually embed change in your life.

What about the *spiritual perspective*?

As we explore the spiritual perspective of why the same thing keeps happening, I invite you to remember three things:

1. **The negativity in your life is happening for a reason**
2. **It relates to your past**
3. **It should not be seen as a bad thing**

If you could detach yourself and be an observer of your own life, you would see that there are patterns and themes to your thoughts; patterns and themes to your behavior; patterns and themes to the feelings and emotions you experience; patterns and themes to your self-talk and so on.

These patterns and themes are unique to you in your soul's journey and they are unique to you in the way you experience your life. In fact they were originally constructed as a unique language that only you would understand and be able to translate. However, due to the intensity and thickness of the *Veil* it has been necessary for spiritual translators to provide support and help you decipher your code e.g. counselors, therapists, coaches, soul contract readers, light workers, healers, etc.

Your patterns and themes are woven throughout your life in how you think, feel, play, interact, make decisions, make choices and in the people you spend your time with. In essence they have helped determine your character, your personality and as a result, the reality you currently experience called your life.

The patterns and themes are there for the sole reason to help you to decipher your Ego's Code, so that you can experience the contrasts and wonderful perspectives of what it means to be a human being so that you can live your true purpose – to be you. You were never meant to 'live' in the uncertainty, frustration, turmoil or pain you may experience.

As a reminder, it is your divine Ego Self that is encoded, for want of a better description, with the patterns and themes you need to decipher and understand.

The True Purpose of Ego

The role of your Ego is that of an educator, a playmate and a partner who has contracted to help you to become the best of who you are and live your best life, rather than as the 'enemy within' which it is so often referred to.

Let me explain. Think of two sports personalities that were adversaries e.g. Muhammad Ali vs. Joe Frazier from boxing or Martina Navratilova vs. Steffi Graff from tennis. Whilst there was a rivalry between them, they challenged each other, they stretched each other, brought the best out of each other and they made each other great! I invite you to see your Ego Self from this perspective – its purpose is to challenge you, to stretch you, to bring the best out of you and to make you great! Remember the meaning of Ego is **E**xpand your **G**reatness **O**ut.

The Formation of Your Ego

We briefly touched on this in Chapter 1, and now we will revisit it in more detail.

You are a divine being, with a divine soul, that has experienced many lifetimes. As part of your past life experiences you were confronted by traumas of differing degrees and magnitude - some minor, some extreme. As you experienced each trauma it created a tear within your soul and part of your soul left and went to a place where it felt safe in the global consciousness.

Often when I am working with people, they will say to me, "It's like part of me is missing" or "I know there is something wrong, I just can't put my finger on it" or "I just feel sad but I don't know why" or something similar. What you need to understand is that this piece of soul is part of your divine essence and you need it.

When your piece of soul left, it created a void (or a hole) in your soul, and the void became filled with energy - all different kinds of negative energy associated with the trauma – self-talk, thoughts, feelings, emotions, behaviors, actions, memories, etc. (see illustration 16). Your life lessons relate to the learning associated with this negative energy and your Ego will attract situations and people to you that will enable you to clear the void of this energy so your lost soul can return to you and reintegrate, making you whole.

71

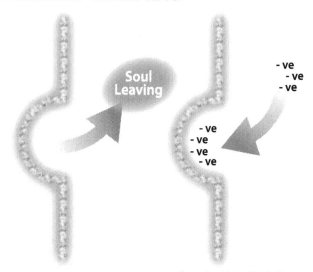

Illustration 16 - *The Void in Your Soul*

The length of the time it takes from when you lost the piece of your soul to the point it returns is driven by you. It can be as short or as long as you choose, but the longer it takes (which for some people has been lifetimes), the bigger the void will become because of each new current lifetime trauma having a similar impact on the void and soul. So what was once a minor trauma with a minor tear (or hole), could now be a major tear (or large hole) because the energies have not been cleared, but have instead compounded.

So how was your Ego formed?

At the point of incarnation, part of your divine Higher Self detaches to form your Ego Self. The ratio is normally about 99% to 1% respectively depending on your soul's journey. Your Ego Self then becomes imprinted with all the lessons you need to learn associated with the traumas of your past.

Your Ego then acts like a purposeful beacon device designed to attract attention to you through the combined energetic frequencies, your negative self-talk, thoughts, feelings, emotions, behaviors, actions, memories, etc. so that you can learn. And it continues to do that until you raise your awareness, pay attention to you, notice what is going on, learn the lessons and release the energy or you die – whichever comes sooner! I call this the **Spiral Effect.**

Here's what it looks like and how it works.

The Spiral Effect

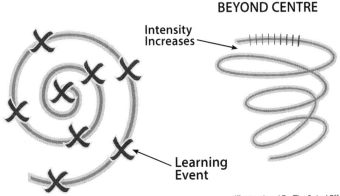

Illustration 17 - *The Spiral Effect*

For each life lesson, your Ego Self will attract a situation, person or people to you so that you can learn – let's call this Event 1. Event 1 could just be a gentle nudge and can take place at birth, childhood, pre-teen, adolescence, or early 20s. If, unfortunately, you don't notice the event, then on another occasion a second event will take place. Let's call this Event 2. Again, if unfortunately, you don't notice this event, then on another occasion a third event will take place, and then a fourth, fifth, sixth and so on. With each event your Ego Self will turn up the intensity to get you to notice and own what is going on for you.

73

If you imagine a spiral (like the illustration above), the closer you get to the center of the spiral the more significant the impact it will have on you and your life e.g. divorce, bankruptcy, redundancy. The point to note is that depending on the soul's journey, the events can be spread over an entire lifetime or accelerated.

But it does not end there... it is possible to fall through the center of the spiral.

If someone falls through the center of the spiral, the intensity level of negativity can reach extremes with non-stop internal chatter, bombarding negative thoughts, constantly feeling sad, miserable, depressed, so much so, that some people reach for drugs, alcohol, food or other vices to numb the pain, to quiet the noise, to soothe, but unfortunately some people do feel they are losing control, reaching burnout or a breaking point and commit suicide or have suicidal thoughts.

The crucial point here that I discovered on my journey deciphering my Ego's Code is that you do not need to learn the lesson consciously; you just need to notice the event, the pattern or theme and release the energy. How amazing is that?!

As a result of the above, a lot of people turn to personal development courses, self-help books, and motivational speakers searching for answers to their problems because these sources profess to have found the solution to a fulfilled life – a magic bullet – for want of a better description. Such sources may help you find part of the answer and part of the solution to that which you seek, but the only true way is to get to know and understand "the guy in the glass" staring back at you each and every morning, it is to get to know you. It is YOU and only YOU that is the true magic bullet.

74

In fact, that is exactly what I, along with other authors and speakers have already done, which is why we share our stories, because we have taken the time to understand what is right for us and works for us as individuals. It is from this point we can then start to help others, but with a caveat. As you read this book (or other books), listen to speakers. etc. it is so critically important that you raise your awareness and take away what works for you. If you are ever unsure, just try it on for size, work with it for a while and then decide.

I have a great friend who I will call Mr. Adventurer (Mr. A). Mr. A travelled the world, climbing mountains, racing across deserts, sailing across oceans and having a fantastic time and breath-taking life. I asked Mr. A why he spent so much time away from home, his family, and his friends on these incredible adventures. He said that he was in search of himself. I asked if he ever found what he was looking for. He said that he had a huge light bulb moment when he was last at home. He was watching his daughter playing and realized that everything that he had been looking for on his travels, he had been carrying around with him all the time, specifically the complete, unconditional, all-encompassing love from his wife, the sound of his children laughing and playing, a life full of endless possibilities, money to make a difference, friends who he loved being with and above all else acceptance from himself, of who he is. He now enjoys his adventures with his family from home. He has never regretted the time he spent away from his family because he said his adventures opened his eyes and opened his heart to appreciate who he is and what he has. This in turn helped him to accept himself and share the love he showers so unconditionally on others, with himself. Seeking adventure or being adventurous is not bad or wrong. What is key is to really understand you and why you are an adventurer. In a lot of ways we are all on a great adventure together, venturing into the unknown, discovering who we are and what living a purposeful and fulfilled life is for each one of us.

Duality & the Divine
Spiritual System

PREVIOUSLY I explained the reasons why you keep experiencing the same thing(s) over and over again. We looked at both the physical and spiritual perspective. By looking at both perspectives separately, I may have given you the impression that they are separate and they operate in your life separately, when in fact this is not true.

When we discussed the formation of the Ego and its role compared to the Higher Self, again, I may have given you the impression that they are separate and operate separately in your life, and again this is not true.

There is a concept in spirituality which talks about something similar called 'duality.' The concept comes from the stance that the Ego is separate from the Higher Self and duality takes place when a person lives from their Ego or lives from their Higher Self. However, one does not and cannot exist without the other because they are the same thing. Furthermore, together they form the essence of what it means for you to be a human being. Therefore, because they are one and the same thing, by definition there cannot be any separateness. Duality being distinct from *dualism* is a myth. *Dualism* is the belief of the great complement or conflict between kindness and being unkind, between good and evil, between yin and yang, between benevolence and malevolence. Dualism exists in our world and implies that there are two moral opposites at work, which we see, and experience around us, every day.

Your physical self has different features and characteristics from your spiritual, divine self, but they cannot and do not operate without having an effect on each other. For want of a better description, they are entwined.

Similarly, your Ego Self may have different features and characteristics in the role that it plays in your life compared to that of your Divine Higher Self, but again, because they are born out of each other and they are eternally connected, one will always impact on the other.

Finally, your physical self and your spiritual self cannot operate without automatically having a significant impact on the reality you call your life. It is not possible for this not to happen. Therefore, whatever life experiences you had yesterday, the day before that, and today, is a direct result of their interaction and in the majority of cases you will be reliving and re-experiencing your past – good or bad – all of which is driven by your self-talk, thoughts, feelings, emotions, actions, behaviors, etc.

Therefore as you learn your lessons from your Ego Self, heal your soul and release the energy, four very distinct things happen:

1. Your Ego Self starts to shrink and your Higher Self grows as your Ego morphs back to being the Higher Self allowing you to Expand your Greatness Out even more, i.e. once you heal and release the energy you have learned or understood the learning you will not repeat the Ego's lesson.

2. The piece(s) of soul you lost from your past life and current life trauma(s) return and reintegrate because you have understood the learning.

3. In your physical body, you create and fire new neural networks in your brain, redesigning your personality to become more aligned to your divine essence and true purpose, i.e. in your brain, sustaining these new thoughts leads to new actions and new behaviors which updates to a newer version of you. It's like you are redesigning your personality by taking all the best parts of you and all your learnings.

4. You may question this, so let's test it. Remember a time in the past where you used to play out a behavior or a way of being, something that today you would never dream of doing or it may be something you want to stop doing now. For example, I used to binge eat chocolate, chips and cookies. When I used to binge eat, it was mostly unconscious and out of my awareness, but I knew that I wanted to stop and make a change.

5. The impact of points 1, 2 and 3 are so significant that the energetic vibration of your self-talk, thoughts, feelings, emotions, actions, behaviors, choices, etc. changes and expands such that your life and all that you experience also starts to change to become more aligned to your new personality.

Why? Because *everything* is *connected* in what is called the **Divine Spiritual System**.

In this final section of Part 1, we are going to look more closely at the Divine Spiritual System, specifically at the interaction between your Ego Self, Higher Self, Physical Self and your reality. Then in Part 2, I will share with you a step-by-step approach to start deciphering your Ego's Code, so that you can experience the best of you and start living your best life.

The interaction between the Ego Self and Higher Self

Pause for a moment and reflect on how you go about finding solutions to the problems or challenges you have in your life.

Some people try to think up or think their way to a solution. I have heard many clients say many times, *"The harder I try to think of a solution the harder it is to find. It just keeps eluding me."*

This is because as Einstein once said, *"We cannot solve our problems with the same level of thinking that created them."*

Illustration 18 - *Head Ruling the Heart*

Others will allow their "heart" to rule their head. They will keep taking the same action over and over again, because as I have heard many times, "I just know in my heart it's right" but they keep getting the same result – the result they don't want!

As Tony Robbins once said, *"If you do what you've always done, you'll get what you've always gotten."*

Illustration 19 - *Heart Ruling the Head*

If you come from the stance that the themes of your life lessons are entwined into every aspect of our life, then in isolation either approach to finding solutions to your problems will only provide part of the answer to the whole. This is because, as we have already discussed, your Ego is imprinted with the lessons that need to be learned in life, with your Higher Self holding the answers. Therefore if you solely use your head ignoring your heart or you blindly follow your heart ignoring your head you will never find the true answer that fulfills you. You are more likely to have the sensation of going around in circles or treading water, never truly moving forward, as you want to.

Furthermore, when you only use your head, or you only use your heart, you get in your own way and make some part of you wrong. Consequently, you are massively discounting and dismissing some of who you are and the benefits of this are lost.

For clarity, it is not one or the other, it is always both that matters.

Illustration 20 - *Unity between the Heart and Head*

In all your life decisions and choices you need to aim for unity between the Ego Self and Higher Self, unity between your human self and your being self, and unity between your head and your heart because when there is unity there is oneness. For want of a better description the head and the heart (Ego Self and Higher Self) MUST work together in tandem, as a partnership, from a place of your intuitive truth. This is the true definition of what it means to be a Human Being.

> **What is oneness?** *Oneness is about aligning and being in unity with your true, natural self and all that is natural in the world. When you are in oneness you are part of something that is beyond you. There is a feeling of perfect harmony and purpose in life. In oneness you can feel such freedom that you access sources of energy, creativity and inspiration that might not otherwise be available. In oneness there is equality and unconditional sharing with others. In essence you have moved through the "I" to the "one."*

In the above paragraph, I have inferred an association between your Human Self, Ego Self and your head (or mind), and a similar association between your Being, your Higher Self and your heart. This is true because this is what it means to be a Human Being.

How do you know when you are in your head, in your heart or in unity? To answer this question, you need to understand the spiritual characteristics of what it means to be a Human Being.

Human Characteristics

Your Human Self

- Is where your Ego resides
- Represents just the 1% of who you are
- Is restricted and restrained by its physical form and capabilities. Even the most talented acrobat who can do incredible things with their body, bending it this way and that like they are elastic, are still restricted
- Is head driven
- Vibrates through the Solar Plexus (also known as the Ego Center)
- Lives in the past and relives your past life and current life traumas over and over again until the lessons are learned
- Communicates through negative self-talk, thoughts, feelings, emotions, actions and behaviors and hence has low energetic vibrations
- Is preoccupied by the 1% of what is missing in your life

- Is focused on repetitive short-term fixes where fulfillment is temporary and eventually wears off
- Has the 'perception' of control, when actually it has relinquished control to outside forces, situations, people, perceptions and circumstances
- Is reactive in nature
- Tends to blame others, rather than take ownership and responsibility
- Is programmed and imprinted with your life lessons

Being Characteristics

Your Being

- Is where your Higher Self resides
- Represents the 99% of who you are and is the purest expression of you
- Is nonphysical and omnipresent
- Is endless, has no boundaries or restrictive patterns
- Is heart driven
- Vibrates through the heart center
- Lives in your truth
- Communicates through positive self-talk, thoughts, feelings, emotions, actions and behaviors and hence has high energetic vibrations
- Is programmed and imprinted with knowledge and wisdom that holds the answers to your true purpose and life lessons
- Is proactive and responsive in nature
- Takes ownership and responsibility for self
- Is focused on you experiencing long-term fulfillment and joy that is sustainable.

Algiz

Algiz is the rune of the Higher Self. Focus on the symbol of Algiz to work with your Higher Self and access your true heart's desire. Algiz will also bring protection and boundaries so that you can honor you and be true to who you are.

Unity and Intuitive Truth

Intuition is a sign when you are experiencing unity and intuitive truth. It is also a sign of you trusting you and when you are in flow.

When I ask my corporate clients or participants on my events, where they feel intuition in their body, they either point to their heart or to their solar plexus. In essence they are experiencing what it means to be 'one' and in flow. When asked what it feels like, they consistently say it just feels right. What is happening energetically is that both the heart center and solar plexus (Ego center) are vibrating simultaneously.

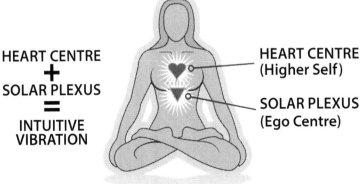

HEART CENTRE
+
SOLAR PLEXUS
=
INTUITIVE
VIBRATION

HEART CENTRE
(Higher Self)

SOLAR PLEXUS
(Ego Centre)

Illustration 21 - *Intuitive Vibration*

85

So, yes, it is possible for you to experience bouts of temporary wholeness or oneness. These are the breadcrumbs from your divine spiritual self that lead you to your truth. It is the consistency and full integration that is the challenge.

How do you know if you are in unity? If you look at the spelling of the word "truth", you will see in the middle is a second word t-**RUT**-h. Whenever there is a problem in your life that does not feel good, or it feels that something is blocking your path you will experience negativity. When you experience negativity of any kind, you are in a RUT, and if you are in a RUT you are not in your truth, and if you are not in truth you are not in unity. It is at this point you need to raise your awareness and pay attention because you are reliving an echo or whisper from your past.

From now on, I invite you to see your RUTs as an opportunity for you to start living your truth.

Power Animal – *The Elephant*

One of the most incredible features of the elephant is its trunk. As the elephant has fairly poor eyesight, it has to rely on and trust its sense of smell. Focus on the elephant to trust your nose, i.e. to trust your instincts and build your intuitive truth so that you completely trust you and your intuition. Remember when you don't trust your intuition, it could come back to bite you in the backside.

The Divine Spiritual System

Everything is connected. Everything is energy. Everything has a frequency of vibration.

Imagine if you will, a fine web that connects all things, including everything you can see, feel, hear, smell and touch together. The web is so fine that you cannot physically see it, but it is there! Just because you cannot see it, does not mean it doesn't exist. Take electricity as an example, it brings power and light, you cannot physically see it, but you know that when you press the light switch, the light will come on or when you plug in the kettle, the water will boil.

Illustration 22 - *The Divine Spiritual System*

The divine spiritual system is very straightforward and very simple. It has just one rule...

There is no "no" in the system, which means, that whatever you send out, you will receive.

And because of this rule, your thoughts have consequences both good and bad. Your feelings have consequences, good and bad. Your self-talk has consequences, good and bad. Your actions have consequences, good and bad and so on.

Why is this so important for you to know?

Remember your ego acts like a beacon sending out signals into the web to attract people, situations and circumstances to you so that you can learn. All your self-talk, your thoughts, your feelings, your emotions, the actions you take, how you behave, and the choices you make all individually have a frequency of vibration which together send out a unique signal that attracts back to you exactly what you send out.

For example, if your thoughts + your self-talk + your feelings + your behavior = I feel bad, then that is exactly what you will experience and on a physical level in your body you will continue to consolidate your existing neural pathways in your brain. So if you send out negativity you will attract back negativity and you will continue to do this over and over and over again, until you change something in your equation of what it means to feel bad.

Your Ego only accounts for just 1% of who you are, but because the neural pathways in your brain are so strong, there is a perception that it is bigger because of your focus. When you focus all your attention here, it feels like that is all there is. What if your Higher Self, which accounts for 99% of you, could also act as a beacon? Better still, what if your Ego and Higher Self worked together with your physical self and you sent out a signal that was 100% of your intuitive truth, what impact would that have on your personality and your life? The mind boggles because when your thoughts + your self-talk + your feelings + your behavior = I feel good or amazing or wonderful, or fulfilled or joyful or happy, then that is exactly what you will experience. You have the power within you to do this irrespective of your life conditions.

Other People's Ego

So far we have only considered your Ego's Code, but every person you know and interact with has their own code to decipher.

Why is this important and why do you need to be aware of it?

Like you, their Ego also acts as a beacon sending out a signal and when there is a vibrational or frequency match to that signal, it will attract similar types of people together. A word of caution, the people attracted to you will either serve you or hinder you. Like you, they have lessons to learn and you can really help and support each other, however, there is also a danger that you can keep each other 'stuck' in the past. What do I mean? You may have heard the term "Naysayers." A Naysayer is someone that when you have an idea which could or would improve your life, they put it down, undermine it, and say things like, "Oh, what do you want to do that for?" to keep you exactly where you are. Now there are two ways to look at this. Their intention could be to keep you stuck (or themselves stuck) because they don't like change, or it could be a gift that has been brought to you to get you to voice your opinion, share your thoughts and speak your truth. Or will you, like in your past, say nothing and stay where you are?

Spiritually, as you learn, heal your past and release the old negative patterns, your energy vibration will change. It will expand out and grow. This means that people who do not serve you will be a vibrational mismatch and will naturally leave your life creating space for you to attract new people, who will be a vibrational match to you. On a biological level, old neural networks will start to fade away as you start to create and fire new neural networks changing your personality.

EXERCISE 7

Characteristics of My Best Friend

In your notebook or on a piece of paper, write down all the characteristics of what you imagine a true best friend would have. What qualities would they have? What do they value? Who do they value? Who are their heroes? How do they speak to you? How do they treat you? How do they treat other people you care about? What do they say about you when you are not there? When you are out of flow, what do they say? What do they do? How do they treat you?

With your list of characteristics, compare them to your current group of friends. How do they compare? If they match, that's great! If they don't, what are you going to do about it?

Special Egos

There are certain people in your life, which you chose at incarnation as 'life' partners to help you to learn and heal your past. They are people who will 'walk with you' throughout your life. They have agreed to specific roles and specific responsibilities. They include your parents or stepparents, family members, spouses and children.

I have heard many people say in many different environments, that they don't like their family, or certain members of their family or their parents. Sometimes, people even become estranged from them. So often, I have heard people say, "Thank goodness I can choose my friends, because I did not choose my family." Well, that is not true. You did choose them and for very good reason.

So if you blame them for the way you are or the way you turned out, how about you pause and thank them because unbeknown to them their Ego and Higher Self played a certain part in your life to help you to learn, to grow, and to heal. You are the way you are because of many reasons. Only one is because their divine self agreed, before you were born, to help you fulfill some lesson(s).

Sometimes when the people around us behave well, they are role modeling for us how to be in the world and when others are behaving badly or in an unacceptable way, they are giving us a strong lesson of "this is NOT how to behave in the world." You can choose. Maybe these lessons are part of your path in this lifetime to heal and help others learn from your experience. Or maybe it will cause you to leave a change in the world... a legacy for now and the future generations to start something good or stop something terrible forever.

If we reflect back to the Veil of Uncertainty, we could say they did get it right, because they did everything you asked of them before you came here – good or bad, painful or not, horrendous or honorable. All you have experienced from them has contributed to the way you are. It has not made you who you are completely; you also need to consider the impact of your past lives as well.

Friends are another group of special egos, but unlike those described above may not be part of your entire life journey. My wife and I regularly say friends are with us for a season, reason or a lifetime.

When I reflect on my life, I can say that most of the friends who have touched my life have been for long seasons or a reason. As I get older now, I am hopeful that my current close friends will be with me for a lifetime.

Finally, because friends come into your life for a season, reason or lifetime, they are also an amazing gift to help identify themes for you to learn from.

PART TWO:

ALIGNING TO YOUR TRUTH
- DECIPHER YOUR CODE!

Understand the truth behind your negativity!

Learn how to decipher your code…
…and stop sabotaging your success!

Living in Flow

TO LIVE in flow, means living in unity. In all situations, circumstances and experiences, you are being true to yourself. In other words, you do what is right for you from your highest good. In Chapter 1, you completed the exercise "Who are you being when you are being you?" This exercise would have given you an insight into what this looks like, sounds like, and feels like to you, but as we have already discovered through our exploration of Part 1, this is more challenging than it first seems, otherwise we would all be doing it already.

In the next few chapters, you will go on a journey to your truth and throughout this journey I want you to ask yourself one question, over and over again:

Am I acting for my highest good?

As you live your life more and more in accordance with your truth, you will meet people who are of a lower energetic vibration to challenge you, to test your commitment to you – these are your Naysayers. In your life, there will always be people who love what you do, disagree with what you do or sit on the fence. As long as you act for your highest good you will always feel fulfilled! If someone else does not like what you are saying or doing, as long as you are doing the right thing for you (for your highest good) and you know that you are taking care of you, then that is someone else's stuff to deal with, and not yours.

By definition as long as you are *genuinely* acting for the highest good, it means that you will automatically be acting for the highest good of others; you will in essence be giving those naysayers an opportunity for them to learn from their Ego and yours.

You are evolving... from the student to the teacher... from fox energy to wolf energy.

Power Animals – *The Fox and the Wolf*

Those people who experience fox energy have so much to contribute, but they sit in the shadows, come out every now and then contribute something magnificent, that adds huge value, and changes the direction of a conversation for the better and then they go back into the shadows. They are learning that their voice matters, that their thoughts matter and that they can make a difference. Fox energy is the energy of the student.

When someone is in wolf energy they have learned to trust their judgment, to trust their intuitive truth and

96

*are willing to step out from the shadows permanently;
to take center stage and be a beacon or example in the
world for people to learn from and aspire to become.
Wolf energy is the energy of the teacher.*

*One is not better than the other. Both are perfect in the
moment. It is an evolution from one to the other.*

Living in Flow does not mean that everything will be easy. Often the journey to living your truth, experiencing your dreams, being successful, finding your perfect job, and meeting your soul mate does not take you in a straight line. More often than not, it looks more like this:

Illustration 23 - *Journey to Your Desired Outcome*

What Living in Flow does do, is it puts you in the driving seat of your life! It stops you from living in the past, but instead your past acts like a reference library of great learning, a place where you can visit when needed consciously and by choice rather than being stuck there repeating old patterns over and over again. Living in flow, means that your life is full of opportunity, clarity, certainty and understanding about who you are and what you consciously choose to experience in your life, *for you.* Living in flow, means that when life throws you a curve ball, a challenge, or an obstacle, you just embrace it and use it to your advantage because you know there is always a solution, a way around it, over it, under it or even through it – there simply is no overwhelm, no anxiety and no fear.

Focus on the symbol of the rune Eihwaz to help you find solutions to overcome blockages and obstacles in your life.

Eihwaz

Focus on the energy of Eihwaz to find the power to find solutions to blockages and obstacles in your life. Know there is always a solution, even in pausing to reflect on your next course of action. Eihwaz will also help develop an aversion to the behavior that causes stress in your life, to help you focus on what matters to you most.

So what is Being True to You? I will answer this for you, but for now the more important question is "What does Being True to You, mean to you?"

What Does Being True to Me, Mean to Me?

As you embark on your journey to your truth, it is so important for you to understand what being true to you means to you, as a benchmark to measure against and to build upon. In your notebook or on a piece of paper, describe what your life will be like, when you are being true to yourself, for your highest good of all.

EXERCISE 8

We live in an egocentric world where we have been pro-grammed and conditioned to think we need to have x, y, z so that we can do everything we want to do, before we can be everything that we want to be, so much so that we don't really know or understand what joy, happiness and fulfillment truly means to us. For example, so many times I have heard people say, "If I just get that job, I will be happy", "When I meet my twin flame soul mate I will feel loved", "If I close that deal I will have all the money I need to do everything I want to do and then I will feel free." In other words, *the route to happiness is external.*

This is *not* being true to you. This is focusing on the 1% of everything that you perceive to be missing from your life, so that you can experience a temporary positive feeling that will eventually fade.

Being True to You is about living through the 100% of the unity of both your Higher Self and Ego Self combined so that you experience the long lasting sustainable joy, happiness and fulfillment in all areas of your life.

My philosophy of *Being True to You* is the opposite of what has been described above; it has four layers and a triple twist!

LAYER 1 – *Unified Being*

Illustration 24 - *Unified Being*

Unified Being is about creating a solid foundation for you in your life! It is all about you being you 100% of the time no matter what!

It is no longer about being someone you think you should be to please others or someone everyone else thinks you should be, and it's no longer about leaving your personality at the door before you go into a meeting. The last example relates to a real situation about what was *told* to a room of graduates and me on day 1 when I started a new career years ago. The Managing Partner said to the room, and I quote, "Our clients are not interested in your personality. They are only interested in your knowledge. You will check your personality at the door!" Today, I work with this same firm of accountants helping them to bring more of their whole self into the workplace. It's interesting how times change!

Unified Being involves you truly noticing you, listening to you, understanding what makes you tick and clearing your mind, your body, your heart and your soul of all unwanted negativity.

Unified Being is also about respecting the 'Guy in the Glass.' You cannot and should not expect anyone else to respect you, until you do this for yourself FIRST!

Raido

Raido is about responsible right action towards you and towards other people. Focus on the symbol of Raido to help you take ownership and responsibility of you, for you. Start by being kind to you, caring for you and showing yourself respect. This includes the foods you eat, how you nurture yourself, how you treat yourself when you see yourself in the mirror and not walking past the mistreatment of you by others. Raido will help you unite you, with you i.e. your Ego Self and your Higher Self.

Values

One of the best ways to truly start getting to know who you are in unity is by understanding your core values.

So, what are values? Consistently on my events, participants have described values as the *things* in your life that are important to you or the *things* that really matter and because they are the *things* you value, by definition they are positive. But values are not things, because things would include belongings, possessions, property, money, even people, i.e. what you have. But what would happen if all you have disappeared tomorrow and all that was left was you? Your core values go deeper than that. They are an intrinsic and deep-rooted part of you. I like to describe them as your moral compass by which you make decisions in your life and navigate your life; they help to distinguish between what is right and what is wrong.

The things you have are a means to an end. It is the feeling that the belongings, the possessions, the property, the money and the people you share your life with that is the value.

For example: When I facilitate a values elicitation exercise I ask people what is important to them. Nine times out of ten they will instinctively say 'family.' But whilst they value family, it is what family gives to them that they truly value at their core. When asked what 'family' gives them, their responses regularly include *love, security, joy, fun, play, challenge, and growth* just to name a few. It is these high energy, high vibrational words that are the core value because they instinctively come from the core of who you are in your unified intuitive truth.

Where do values come from? There has been a lot of research done on this over the years and there are a lot of theories. I like to keep things simple, straightforward and easy to understand. To me values come from two sources – **learned** values and values you are **born with.**

Learned values are those values you have learned in your current lifetime. They are values you would have copied from parental figures e.g. parents, grandparents, teachers, bosses, peer groups, etc. and those you have learned for yourself from your life experiences to date.

Born or pre-birth values are values you have brought with you from previous lifetimes. They also include spiritual values embedded in your divine Higher Self.

Both are very important but you do NOT need to know which is which. What you do need to know is as follows:

Within your physical body, both sets of values are currently hardwired into your neurology, which means that when they are honored you will unconsciously fire together neural pathways that are wired together, consolidating the value and positive experience. But equally when your values are dishonored the negativity associated with the lessons you need to learn will also fire the neural pathways that are wired together, consolidating the past lessons into the now causing you to repeat old values, relive the past and experience negativity. In life, the latter is what happens a lot of the time because people do not consciously know their values. This means that you could be living your life like a game of chance focusing on the 1% of what you perceive is missing and dishonoring your values over and over again.

Knowing your values means that you can consciously choose to experience the positivity of honoring your values over and over again. It also means that you can consciously choose to change them if you wish. Your values are also entwined with your life lessons so as you learn the lessons, and release the energy of the past, you will have new thoughts and as you will recall, your new thoughts will create new neural pathways literally changing your brain. As a result, you may need to update the values by which you choose to live your life by, to consistently fire your newly wired neural pathways, to ensure that you consistently honor the new you and new life you have designed for yourself.

The starting place is for you to consciously understand your values.

My Values

On page 185 you will find my values elicitation exercise for you to complete. There are 8 steps. The exercise can take as short as 45 minutes or as long as 3 hours. It is up to you. The longer it takes the more information you have about you to work with in your life. However, in my experience the quicker you can do this exercise, the better as I have found over many years that your first and quickest response gives the best results.

For all the reasons described above, please give yourself the gift of completing this exercise.

EXERCISE 9

As you will probably now appreciate, this whole book is about your *Unified Being* because it is about you getting to truly know you. As you work through the exercises and embark on your journey to your truth this is exactly what will happen in ways that you can only imagine at this moment in time.

LAYER 2 – *Enjoyment of Your Life*

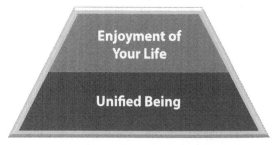

Illustration 25 - *Enjoyment of Your Life*

Through being yourself, you will naturally discover your true path and direction in life. The more you get to know you, the more you will discover and align to what you love in life and be able to design a life that honors you, and truly makes your heart sing rather than forcing parts of your life to fit who you *think* you are. That is what layer 2 is all about – The Enjoyment of Your Life.

There are two runes that will help you design the life you want for you at layer two – Fehu and Wunjo.

Fehu

Fehu is the rune of fulfilment. Focusing on the symbol of Fehu will help with your nourishment from the most worldly to the sacred and divine. Fehu invites you to reflect with carefulness as to what fulfilment actually means to you and your wellbeing. Fehu also invites you to think about how you wish to share your fulfilment because the mark of the divine self is the ability and willingness to nourish others.

Wunjo

Wunjo is the rune of Ecstatic Joy. Focusing on the symbol of Wunjo will bring in new energy, energy that may have become blocked before now. Similarly to Fehu, Wunjo invites you to reflect on what a joyful life experience would look like, sound like and feel like to you. Wunjo is a rune of restoration of the self becoming aligned with the intuitive self and will bring new clarity of plans, goals, dreams and ambitions.

My Fulfilment and Joy

This is a fun exercise that can be done in more than one way. The first is to take a large blank sheet of paper and then draw or paint a picture of what a fulfilled and joyful life means to you.

OPTION 2, *record a Mind Movie of your fulfilled and joyful life by going to MindMovies.com.*

OPTION 3, *record a song or poem or a story of your life that you can tell yourself.*

OPTION 4, *could be a combination of the above or something completely different. You must choose what is right for you.*

EXERCISE 10

Whichever option you choose, the important thing is to use the output at least twice every day (once in the morning when you wake up, and once just before you go to sleep at night). By looking at your picture, or watching your Mind Movie or listening to your song, poem or story, the repetition will start to create new thoughts, new feelings, new behaviors and new experiences in your life. This is because, the repetition and consistency changes your brain by creating new neural pathways, which change your personality and hence the life you live. On a spiritual level, the energy from past trauma(s) is being released and you are experiencing the healing in the here and now.

Power Animal – *The Dolphin*

If you are holding your breath or holding your self back, focus on the dolphin to breathe new life into you.   The dolphins can help you get outside, to play, to have fun, to enjoy yourself, and most of all breathe life into you.

It is these first two layers *together* that will bring you closer to living consistently through your intuitive truth as well as a refreshed sense of wow, confidence and inner knowing about who you are in your life, i.e. that your route and source to happiness is internal, but it doesn't end there...

Here comes the first twist!

LAYER 3 – *Unconditional Sharing*

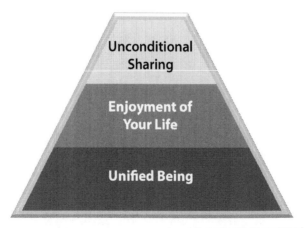

Illustration 26 - *Unconditional Sharing*

When we feel great in ourselves, we are naturally more loving and more caring towards others. We unconditionally (and unconditionally is the keyword here) want other people to feel as great and as happy as we do. We want to share our experiences, share our knowledge and share our happiness and for others to enjoy more fulfilling lives for themselves.

If you pause for a moment and reflect on a time when you unconditionally helped another person how great you felt after taking care of that person. This is a two way street. What happens is they feel happy because they have been taken care of and you feel even happier because you have contributed to their happiness. You have shown them that they matter! You have enhanced their existence and experience of themselves and as a result you have experienced the same for you.

Here comes the second twist!

LAYER 4 – *The By-product*

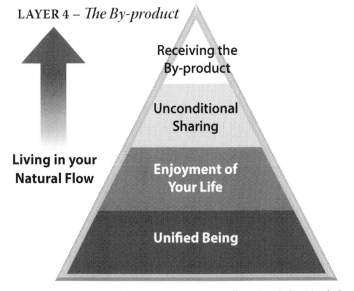

Illustration 27 - *Receiving the By-product*

So by first being yourself, enjoying what comes naturally and doing what makes you happy, helping others, it is then as a by-product only that you actually receive your true heart's desires. *It happens naturally!* The by-product is the life you designed in reality and in action. This is the second twist!

As I said in Part 1, on a spiritual level you do not need to consciously understand your life's lessons. When you set your objective to honor you and shape your life in the right way by living in flow and through unity, the healing takes place naturally!

Here comes the third twist in this beautiful story called your life!

When you look at the above pyramid, the by-product looks so small that I can hear your beautiful ego whispering, "Is it worth it for all that effort?"

Yes it is because the third twist is called **The Realm of Fulfilment!**

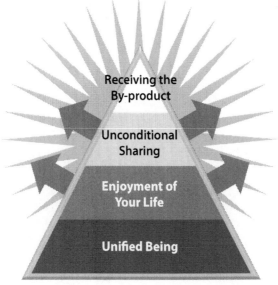

Illustration 28 - *The Realm of Fulfilment*

The realm of fulfilment actually shows that when you live from a Unified Being existence by being true to who you are then your life (the by-product) expands exponentially and is in fact limitless. Furthermore, as you move up through each layer, the boundaries of what you perceive you are capable of being, capable of enjoying and capable of sharing gradually vanish and become limitless and never ending. The intensity of the positive feelings and emotions you experience expand and grow with you. Your energy vibration expands and grows with you. You actually then start to attract everything you want to attract in your life *naturally.* You become a vibrational match to joy and all that brings with it. You experience the life you designed and you experience the very best of who you are. You don't just receive the tip of the pyramid. There is a vibrational and relationship match between how you feel about you and what you are living every day.

> *What is energy vibration?* Imagine tuning a car radio into your favorite radio station. Just like your favorite radio station you have your own unique 'radio' frequency called an energy vibration that you send out into the Divine Spiritual System (The Web) through your thoughts, feelings, emotions, actions, behaviors, and self-talk. The more positive you are, the higher and more positive your frequency. The more negative you are, the lower your frequency.

> *What is a vibrational match?* *Everything is energy and therefore has its own unique 'radio' frequency or energy vibration that it sends out into the Divine Spiritual System (The Web). Just like a magnet, you will be repelled away from people and things that do not have a similar energy vibration to you. A vibrational match takes place when your energy vibration matches and attracts you to people and things that do have the same energy vibration as you.*

ALL layers must be present for you to live a fulfilled and happy life. So the more you know about you and do what makes you happy, the more this will be replicated and show up in your life in terms of your health, your relationships, your career, your finances, and the trust and confidence you have in you. i.e. the more joy you send out into The Web, the more you will experience back to you and ultimately the more fulfilled you will be in life.

The main point to keep in mind is that the opposite is also true. I call this **Living Upside Down** and we will be looking at this in the next Chapter.

Reality Check!

You may be reading this and thinking, "*Yeah Clayton, that's all well and good, but I need to pay the bills and hold down a job; it's not that easy to just 'be' and 'enjoy' what I love.*"

My answer to you is *'I know... I've been there!*" I encourage you to make a start, no matter how small. Do one thing and build from there. It *will* make a difference. In my experience your results may start off small, but they will soon enjoy the snowball effect, i.e. start small and then get bigger and bigger and bigger.

Living Upside Down

AS A shamanic practitioner I have a huge passion for nature and animals. For a moment, think about your favorite animal in the animal kingdom. Like all animals it is guided by and lives its life in accordance with its natural instincts. It goes through life developing, nurturing and harnessing what comes naturally. It does not force itself to do the things it does not want to do, or go against its natural way of being. As a result, it is always connected to divine source energy. Unlike human beings it doesn't experience loss of self or detachment.

> *What is Divine Source Energy?* *There is energy all around you; an energy that flows through you; an energy that is connected to all things everywhere. It is kind, gentle, full of love and very powerful. It is an intelligence that is universal and transcends all human capabilities. It is connected to you, you are*

connected to it and it is filled with infinite possibilities for you to access. I have heard it called many things, - Higher Power, Infinite Intelligence, Gaia, God, Spirit, and Consciousness.

Nature has inspired us, taught us and guided us in many ways, but yet in society we have been conditioned to detach ourselves from nature, to disconnect from what comes naturally, from who we are. When we detach ourselves from life, whether consciously or unconsciously, we detach from our natural self and move away from our truth. As a result you will feel out of balance, out of rhythm, and out of flow. When you experience negativity, these are signals from you, to you, that you are moving out of flow and that you need to make a decision to realign by paying attention to you and noticing what is going on for you in that moment. But if you have been conditioned to automatically ignore it or stuff it down, you are unconsciously choosing to detach from your natural self and to move away from the truth of who you are.

You may as well live your life like a game of chance and take a gamble by shaking a *Magic 8 Ball* to seek advice or throwing *dice* to determine your next course of action, because you will get the same random results.

The Magic 8 Ball is a toy used for fortune-telling or seeking advice

Illustration 29 - *Magic 8 Ball*

112

But why gamble with your life? You may win a few times which will give you a short-lived sense of excitement, but eventually the excitement will become restlessness, your outcomes unsuccessful, and cause feelings of helplessness, guilt, anxiety or even stress. You may even lie to yourself

Illustration 30 - *Throwing Dice*

or to others causing you to lose relationships, sabotage success, gain weight or other patterns, as you get closer and closer to the center of the spiral. This is your Ego in action!

When you ignore you, you are *living upside down*.

Living upside down is living against the flow of your natural self. It's like you're walking around on your hands all day long, every day, 7 days per week. So what would this be like?

Illustration 31 - *Living Upside Down*

In the beginning it may be fun, a novelty with lots of people noticing you, giving you attention, smiling, saying how cool you are, how talented you are, etc. but over time this will eventually stop.

Living upside down you can't take good care of your physical wellbeing, and you can't eat properly so you would lose energy causing you to get tired, frustrated, short tempered and reactive.

Because you are not designed to live permanently walking on your hands, you would get giddy, become off-balance, stumble and constantly be bumping into things.

Finally, you would not be able to see clearly - just feet, ankles and legs all around you.   Not much of an existence really!

Living upside down is *unnatural* and when you experience negativity, without learning and by ignoring you and your needs, you are resisting your life, and battling the tides of the Ego rather than going with its flow, because you are caught in the **tunnel of reaction.**

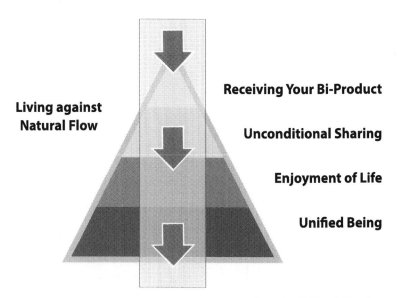

Illustration 32 - *Tunnel of Reaction*

The Tunnel of Reaction

I invite you to notice the differences between the above pyramid compared to the pyramid in the previous chapter on living in flow.

When you are caught in the tunnel of reaction you only ever experience the 1% your life, and you have blinkers on that are selfish and the only focus is on layer 4 - 'Having' so that you can experience a short-term emotional high, that is incongruent to your truth, causing you to be out of balance and out of flow.

Let me be very clear. I am not saying that it is bad or wrong to have money, or to desire material possessions and success because we need money to be in the world, and to live. Some of the most successful people on the planet use their money, success and influence to make a difference e.g., Anthony Robbins, Oprah, Richard Branson and David Beckham just to name a few. The distinction is that their success has become sustainable because in my view, they took the time to get to know who they are, they nurtured their natural talents, healed their past and they live life in alignment with their values. Furthermore, their success did not happen overnight. It was gradual; it grew as they grew, and the more aligned they became to their Unified Being, the fast and bigger it became. Did they make mistakes? Yes, absolutely, but they learned from them and changed their life as a result rather than allowing their mistakes to perpetuate and repeat.

Very rarely does layer 3 'unconditional sharing' show up at all because relationships become superficial rather than meaningful.

You only get to know a fraction of yourself and what makes you tick, therefore you only ever enjoy a small part of what is possible for you in your life. You become conditioned to keep reliving the past, repeating the same 'old' patterns and doing the same things over and over again like an **endless loop of negative learning** ...

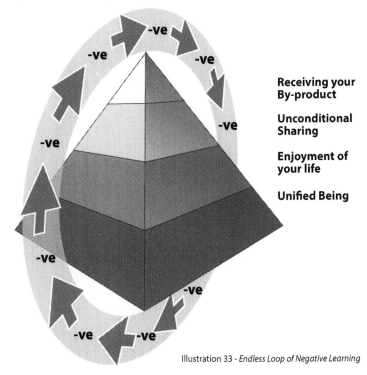

Receiving your
By-product

Unconditional
Sharing

Enjoyment of
your life

Unified Being

Illustration 33 - *Endless Loop of Negative Learning*

... until you break free of your patterns of negativity, by learning the lessons you need to learn and heal the past through the **8 Truths to decipher your code.**

Eight Truths to
Decipher Your Code

DECIDE, COMMIT, SUCCEED - is the strapline and ethos of the company that created my favorite fitness programs called Insanity and Insanity Max30. It is one of the best straplines I have come across for delivering any form of change in my life.

*A **strapline** is an advertising slogan. Its purpose is to emphasize a phrase that a company or person wishes to be remembered about for its product, service or image.*

Both Insanity and Insanity Max30 are 60-day fitness programs. On Day 1 of Insanity, and thereafter every two weeks you do a 20-minute fitness test to see how you are progressing and improving throughout the program. On Day 1, halfway through my fitness test, I ran to the toilet and was sick! It was awful and it was painful. I did not appreciate just how unhealthy and unfit I had become. For the first 20 days of the program, I had a very close relationship with the floor in our living room, but I did not stop and I did not give up. By the end of the program I lost 42 pounds and 6 inches around my waist in 60 days.

I am not sharing this to impress you. I am sharing this to impress upon you what is possible for you in your life when you make a decision to make a change, which you are committed to. In my life this includes unconditional love from my beautiful wife, a loving and caring daughter, complete health, sustainable weight loss, a successful business where I get to use my natural talents, have fun, laugh and play, money in the bank, spirituality and faith, and that's just for starters.

As you decipher your code, the journey to your truth will have ups and downs. It will have curve balls, and you will have choices and decisions to make, but I promise you it will be worth it.

You cannot embark on this journey half-heartedly thinking "I'll give it try", because your Ego, your Higher Self, your mind and your body, will know that you don't really mean it and **nothing will change**. This is because even if you say 'the words' that you are committed, if you remain uncertain, your thoughts, your actions, your behaviors, and your self-talk will all be incongruent to the words that you say, but will be aligned to your true feelings of uncertainty i.e. you will *not* be walking your talk. Consequently, the energy vibration you send out into The Web will not be a vibrational match 'to being committed', but will instead be a vibrational match and attract back to you the 'uncertainty' you truly felt in the first place.

You do have to DECIDE, this is what you want to do, for you.

You do have to COMMIT, that you will take action, for you.

... And then you will be SUCCESSFUL,
in whatever that means to you.

There are eight truths to deciphering your code, which bring eight lessons. Each lesson begins with the letter 'L' to help you remember. I will explain each one in turn.

Truth 1: **You Matter! Take time to get to know you**
Lesson 1: *Look at you, notice you, see you!*

Truth 2: **All the answers you seek lie within**
Lesson 2: *Listen carefully and hear you!*

Truth 3: **You must go into and through the resistance**
Lesson 3: *Learning is the route to being!*

Truth 4: **What is yours will come to you**
Lesson 4: *Let go. Detach. Feel the relief first!*

Truth 5: **Speaking highly of yourself will naturally change your results**
Lesson 5: *Language has energy and power. Think before you speak!*

Truth 6: **Your environment will enable you to flourish or falter**
Lesson 6: *Life conditions and environments contribute to your success!*

Truth 7: **The more you love your life; the more your life will love you**
Lesson 7: *Love your life as a passion!*

Truth 8: **There is always an opportunity for kindness**
Lesson 8: *Love you completely and unconditionally!*

Please note: For each of the eight truths, you are NOT expected to be perfect at any of them. Like when I started Insanity, I just did what I could do. It is the same here. It is progressive. It's like anything, - the more you practice, the better you will become, and guess what? You will create new experiences in your life and therefore wire and fire new neural networks in your brain as a result.

As I go through each of the truths and share the lessons, your beautiful Ego may react to some of what I am going to share. The way that you now start to work with your Ego is with the following steps:

STEP 1: Pay attention!

*STEP 2: Acknowledge and show appreciation
for the reaction!*

*STEP 3: Your awareness and acknowledgement creates
presence, which temporarily moves you from the
past into the here and now.*

*STEP 4: From the 'here and now' you then make a choice –
are you going to react or respond?*

A reaction will flow from your Ego Self, which may escalate a situation and will keep you locked in the endless loop of negative learning. A response is from your intuitive truth, which breaks the pattern, releases energy of the past and enables you to start to heal. The more you repeat new patterns of behavior, old neural networks will fade away and new neural networks will form, changing your brain. Also, the frequency of the Ego's beacon starts to change as it combines with your Higher Self sending out new frequencies into The Web attracting your new life to you.

STEP 5: Having made your choice, take appropriate action.

TRUTH 1 – *You Matter! Take time to get to know you*

The core lesson is...
Look at you, notice you and see you!

I have always found it interesting that the one person we spend 100% of our time with, is often the one person we least know - You. It's like we take ourselves for granted or depending on the stories we tell ourselves, we get pushed down the pecking order of priority in our own lives.

Have you ever wondered why your friends love to spend time with you? Well now is your chance. In my own life, I have regular *Daddy Time* with my daughter and regular *Honey Time* with my wife where we get to spend time *together* and do the things we love *together*. But I noticed that I did not have regular *Me Time*. In fact when my wife asked me what I love to do for *me*, I really struggled to answer the question. It took time for me to come up with a meaningful list. How can you be expected to access the 100% of your divine self, live the dream life your soul craves and all the wonder this has to offer, if you don't spend any time with you?

Truth 1 is about giving you, the gift of you. Spend some time with you. Discover what you love to do; what are your passions, what are your gifts and natural talents, what truly makes your heart sing? Raise your awareness, pay attention and truly notice what is going on inside of you. Take time to understand what you need. Look out for the signs around you and the impact your environment has on how you think, how you feel, how you act, your self-talk and how you treat yourself. These are key components to start experiencing the very best of who you are.

121

The real challenge with Truth 1 is that having a conscious awareness of you is frequently alien because we have often conditioned ourselves to tune out. We tend to live on automatic pilot flitting from one thing to the next. It can feel like something has taken over us and we are in a trance. Furthermore for some people, the thought of spending time with themselves can be very uncomfortable because they have learned how to avoid themselves. It's like their life is a movie and they have only given themselves a small part to play, rather than a leading role. If this is you, start small, but please do start. You will be amazed at the magic inside of you.

Where do you start?

To begin, over the next couple of weeks, I invite you to just start raising your awareness and noticing what makes you happy and what makes you sad. Just setting this as an intention, you will start to notice new things about you. Carry around a journal or use a smartphone or tablet to make notes. Remember, this may be something new for you so be kind to yourself. The purpose of taking notes is so that you can eventually start to identify themes and patterns in your life – positive and negative. When you understand your themes and patterns, you can then consciously choose to start to build on them by doing more of what makes you happy or change them by doing less of what makes you sad.

> **What is an intention?** *An intention is a commitment to carry out an action or actions in the future. It is a desire to achieve certain goals. On a spiritual level intentions are much more powerful than hopes, wishes and wants. Our true intentions release energy into the divine spiritual system (The Web) that makes things happen. Whatever your aims are in your life, when you gather your energies and keep your target in your sights, Source energy will back your vision and bring it to fruition.*

On a spiritual level, spend time with you, notice you and what is going on in your life, and start to release the energy from your past that holds you back. The more you do it, the more you release.

Messages from your Ego

This is where the fun starts. After a couple of weeks of noticing what makes you happy and sad, I invite you to raise your game a little; to sharpen your focus, to notice what is going on inside you – in your thoughts, your feelings, your emotions, how you behave, your self-talk, your reactions and so on. Start with the following:

First thing in the morning when you wake up and start your day, notice how you are feeling, the thoughts you have and what you say to yourself because this will often impact on the rest of your day. If they are negative, just make a note of them. Do not make them right or wrong. They are happening for a reason. If they are positive, again take note.

- **During your days** notice when you specifically experience **negativity**. Note down what you were doing, who you were with, what was said to you, what you said to yourself, the thoughts you had, how it made you feel, how you reacted and how long you felt negative afterwards.

- **During your days** notice when you specifically **enjoyed positive experiences**. Again, note down what you were doing, who you were with, what was said to you, what you said to yourself, the thoughts you had, how it made you feel, how you responded, and how long you felt positive afterwards.

- Finally, **when you go to bed at night** notice how you are feeling, because this will impact on how restful your night's sleep is.

On a daily basis, praise yourself and identify small, quick wins to help you that will start to make a difference, e.g. if you need to be more healthy, drink one more glass of water or eat one more piece fruit or get one more hour of sleep.

After the first week, review your notes and identify any themes or patterns to both your negativity and what you enjoyed doing. If you struggle to see the themes or patterns, pause, sit quietly and breathe. Put your hand on your heart, go inside and ask your divine Higher Self for the answer. Trust your intuitive truth – simply ask the questions, "What is the lesson I need to learn?" "What is the pattern I need to learn from?" As you quiet your mind, you will receive an answer – every time!

If you prefer, you can reach out to a trusted friend, coach, therapist or counselor. Most often the best results come from you being asked questions and gaining the insights yourself through your own filters and life experiences. The best therapists, counselors and coaches will share with you what they are observing from you and ask you great questions to enable you to find the answer for you.

For each theme or pattern identified, the important thing is to decide what *new* action or actions you are going to take to change them. My recommendation is to start small and build up from there. Similarly to the happy and sad exercise above, ask yourself, what are you going to do more of, and what are you going to do less of? Choose one thing, work with it, master it and then add a second, then a third, fourth, etc. For example, your theme or pattern may be that you consistently hold yourself back because you think or tell yourself that you are not good enough. Your action may be to take a small risk and voice your opinion once a day or share your thoughts more often or tell people how you really feel.

Fun and play...!

Getting to know you is not just about immersing yourself in the negativity stuff! It is also about making sure you immerse yourself in the joy of what you love to do.

The very first exercise you completed in this book – "Who are you being, when you are being you" – you wrote answers to the following two questions:

What are you doing when you experience the greatest sense of personal fulfilment?

What are you doing when you experience the greatest sense of joy, peace and happiness?

I invite you to answer the following question...

*What do you love to do for fun and play that supports
the best version of you?*

... And then plan it in – make time for you to meet and experience the best of you.

As part of getting to know you, I invite you to spend more time doing more of the above, and to also ask yourself the questions, "What else? What else do I love to do? What else am I passionate about? What else brings me joy? What else do I love to do for fun? What else do I do to play?"

If your beautiful Ego mind starts to react saying "OMG, I don't have time for that", follow the steps referred to above on page 120.

Messages from your Spirit Guides

I also invite you to start looking outside of yourself for the signs and symbols from your Spirit Guides and from nature.

What are Spirit Guides? Spirit Guides are enlightened beings that act as a guide or protector to human beings. Spirit Guides live as energy or as light beings. They include animal guides, angels, guardians, and family members who have died. Some guides are people who have lived many former lifetimes.

To start with notice:

- **Animals** that consistently cross your path or that you are afraid of. Each animal has a meaning and a message for you. For example, I was seated at my computer working and a ladybug flew in through the window and landed on my computer. This was such a rare experience, something that I had not experienced before, so I had to pay attention. The ladybug is about setting higher goals and setting new heights. This was an amazing gift because I was sitting there planning my goals for the forthcoming year and when I reflected on my goals, they weren't challenging or stretching enough.

When seeking to understand the message from the animals, you can start by researching on the Internet under Power Animals, Animal Spirits or Animal Guides. Alternatively, I can recommend the following two books *Animals Speak* by Ted Andrews and *Medicine Cards* by Jamie Sams and David Carson. Eventually, with practice you should build to speak to your animal guides directly and trust your intuition on the guidance they give to you. My meditation CD *"Meet and learn from your Power Animals"* that supports The Ego's Code, shows you how you can do this for yourself.

Animals that you are afraid of have significant meaning, because they are testing whether you are ready to receive the learning that they bring. Here are two examples of the lessons I learned from my animal guides – a fear of snakes, was about shedding old skins to embrace the transformation brought by a new life; a mouse, was about appreciating the small things in my life and reading the small print before signing a contract.

- **Angelic numbers and messages**. If you wake in the night at the same time over and over again, pay attention! If you are driving down the road and you see the same numbers on a car license plate, pay attention! One day I was driving to a client when

I saw two different cars with the numbers 777 on their license plates, a taxi with the telephone number 777-7777, and one truck with the numbers 777 on its side. I paid attention! This was an amazing gift, because the message means:

"You are definitely on the right path in every area of your life. Stay balanced and spiritually aware so that you can continue moving forward on the illuminated path"
- Source: **Angel Numbers** *by Doreen Virtue*

This is a small pocket-sized and very insightful book I have had for many years. It is really easy to use because all the numbers are in order. It also comes in a downloadable app where you can tap in the numbers for ease of use.

- **In your work** you may find you give the same repetitive advice, insight, recommendation or feedback to a client or co-worker. Again, pay attention as this advice may also be for you. Just last week I was giving a reading to someone. The theme of the reading was about speaking their truth and sharing how they were feeling. Always after my readings I reflect on whether there were any messages for me. I realized there was something that I had been holding back that I had not shared with a family member, so this enabled me to take the right course of action.

In conclusion, you can repeat any or all of the above exercises as often as you wish and check for similar or new themes on a regular basis. However, it is very important to give yourself regular breaks e.g. one day off each week or even take a vacation to rest and rejuvenate, because you need to allow your learning to assimilate, for the energy of the past to be released and new neural networks to form. All of which can take its toll on the physical body and be exhausting. This is why you also need to listen to you, which brings us nicely on to Truth 2.

TRUTH 2 – *All the answers you seek lie within*

The core lesson is...

Listen carefully and hear you!

All the answers you seek lie within, everything else is just decoration.

There is a big difference between listening to you and actually hearing you. When listening it is possible for you to only half listen, to tune out, to become distracted, restless, to avoid what is being said, to become defensive, or come up with excuses, all of which prevent you from actually spending quality time with you and learning about you and your needs in life. Nowadays this is further complicated when we try to multi-task between Twitter, Facebook or texting, but again that inevitably means we are not listening to ourselves, let alone noticing what is going on inside or around us. Inevitably, it's about balance. There are real positive sides to social media too because it is enables you and me to stay in touch and for you to stay connected with friends and family.

Pause for a moment and reflect on what it feels like when other people don't listen to you. Do you feel excluded, unloved, angry, frustrated, sad, unimportant, and invisible like you don't exist? When you don't listen to yourself and hear what is important to you, you are treating yourself exactly the same way. This may be because of some of the stories you tell yourself to keep you safe.

You are the most important person in your life, because without you, you have no life, but do you feel important to you? If not, now is the time to start and you do that by listening to you and actually hearing what you need.

To hear you must be present, because as I said earlier, being present moves you temporarily from the past into the here and now. Being present means being completely with you, centered in you, no distractions, so that you can understand and feel your needs, wishes and heart's desires.

To build and maintain a great relationship with you, to consistently take action for your higher good, and to make you feel better about yourself there are a number of behaviors you can start to do to honor you.

- **Listen closely and seek to hear everything**. You have two ears and one mouth for a reason; you should listen and hear twice as much as you speak (and that includes your internal conversations). Seek to understand before thinking you have understood - ask yourself questions, acknowledge you, your thoughts, your feelings, your needs, and your desires. Being present with you, hearing you, and acknowledging you, shows that you care a lot more than just dismissing, discounting or ignoring you. This is all it takes to start to show you that you are important to you.

- **Have some 'Switch off' time.** Switch off your phone. Switch off your computer. Don't focus on anything else, other than you, even for a moment. You will never be able to connect with you if you are busy connecting with your stuff! Give yourself the gift of your full attention. That is a gift few people ever give themselves.

- Give the same gift to you that you give so many others – **your time**. As human beings we tend to give, give, and give to others at the cost of ourselves, but you deserve it too. Focus on the energy of the rune Gebo to help you receive more of you.

Gebo

Gebo is the rune of giving and receiving. If giving is like breathing out, the more you give, the more you breathe out and breathe out and breathe out and breathe out. At some point you will suffocate unless you breathe in and receive. Give yourself the gift of you, breathe life into your life and receive you.

- **Shine the spotlight on you.** We very rarely praise ourselves for doing something really great. Tell yourself what you do well! This is another way to show you that you care.

- **Be genuine and honest with you.** Honesty is one of the most important things for your success. Having personal awareness to notice what is going on inside and around you is great, but if you cannot be honest with you about your thoughts, your feelings, or what something means to you, then any action you take will be pointless and you will remain in the endless loop of learning.

Messages from your Body

As you know, your Ego acts as a beacon to attract situations, circumstances, people etc. to you to enable you and to enhance the opportunity for you to learn and heal. If you get in your own way by your head ignoring your heart, or you blindly follow your heart or you ignore/stuff down the negativity, you will move closer to the center of the spiral. Then the intensity and the painful impact on your life increase.

One of the ways this can happen is through messages in your body. For example, when you experience a negative feeling such as fear, the energy of fear gets trapped in a certain location in your body depending on the type of fear it is. For me, a fear of moving forward shows up as an ache in my lower left leg. If I am fearful or worried about money, I will experience a pain in the lower left hand side of my back. If I am afraid of not being true to myself, I will experience tightness in my right shoulder and shoulder blade. How do I know? Because I asked the pain what messages it had for me that I needed to learn.

Here's how: Pause, sit quietly and breathe in and out a few times, put your hand on your heart, go inside and ask your divine Higher Self what is the reason you have attracted this ache or this pain or this illness to you? Trust your intuitive truth! Then ask any or all of the following questions: "What is the lesson I need to learn?" "What do you need from me?" "Who benefits from my pain or my illness?" "What does it give me or others time to do?" These questions will help you further uncover your message(s) from your body. You will receive an answer every time.

In addition to negative messages from your body, also listen to positive messages from your body e.g. how your body responds to healthy food, plenty of rest, enjoying something you love, laughter, and music.   It's not always all about the negativity. Like you, your Ego Self loves positivity too because it gets a rest from the negativity.

So in addition to noticing your negativity... listen to your body... you will be amazed what you learn!

TRUTH 3 – *You must go into and through the resistance to Learn*

The core lesson is...
Learning is the route to being!

When it is dark inside a room, it is difficult to see and occasionally we may feel so afraid of the dark that we do not enter.   On the edge of darkness there are shadows of light.   Your Ego Self agreed to live in the darkness of your negativity. However, it does, as you do, experience glimpses of relief from the darkness by the light in the shadow shining from your Higher Self i.e. the wonderment of joy, happiness and fulfilment. This is why it craves to reconnect with the Higher Self because it has experienced the joy, happiness and fulfilment before (when it was part of the Higher Self), and wants to experience it again.

Earlier, we touched on the Shamanic World Tree. **The World Tree** forms an integral part of Shamanic teaching, because it links the world of humanity with the world of spirit. The World Tree is the bridge that connects three worlds, the upper world (divinity and heaven), the middle world (the here and now on earth), and the lower world (the darkness of the Ego Self).

To learn, you must enter the darkness of your lower world. You do this *naturally* by *working with* your Ego Self and learning from your negativity, helping it to permanently reconnect with light of your Higher Self. As you do, your life will transform, but you may feel afraid and experience resistance.

Resistance for want of a better description is an unconscious refusal to own and take responsibility for problems or challenges in your life. There is a famous saying by Carl Jung:

"What you resist, will persist"

To resist means to push against, to oppose or withstand. Hence when your Ego Self invites you to learn from your negativity, if the neural pathways in your brain are wired and conditioned to fire in a way to fight against it, or to ignore it, or to avoid it, or to stuff it down be it a problem or challenge with a relationship, money, your weight, your health, your career or business, etc., then the vibrational frequency you are sending out into The Web (divine spiritual system) is "I don't want to face this" or "I don't want this in my life." But, remember that what you send out into The Web you will receive back and because the divine spiritual system will never say "no" to you, you will receive more and more of what you are focusing your attention on.

So what are the main reasons people resist? The main ones I have come across working with clients and people on my events are as follows:

- **Fear of the unknown**
- **Fear of loss**
- **No reasons to change**
- **Habit**

Your emotional scale – How to work with your negative feelings

It is easy for any human being to understand that *fear* does not feel as good as happiness or joy or unconditional love.

But how many times in your life have you heard family, friends or even colleagues try to give you a positive explanation about what is going on to move your attention, focus and feelings *in that moment* from the negative to the positive.

For some people, moving from feeling *fearful* to *joyful* in one go is too big a leap. Therefore when you are working with your negative feelings, imagine you are travelling by train from the city of 'fear' to the city of 'joy'. As you travel on your journey, you will pass through various other stations one at a time e.g. anger, to courage, to hope, to understanding, to happiness, to love until you eventually arrive in Joy. (See illustration 34 below).

For all your life lessons about money, love, career, success, confidence etc., you will have a unique emotional scale. It is very important for you to understand YOUR emotional journey rather than what other people tell you it should be.

After all, they are your feelings. Otherwise you may not make the progress you deserve or it may take longer to arrive at your desired destination.

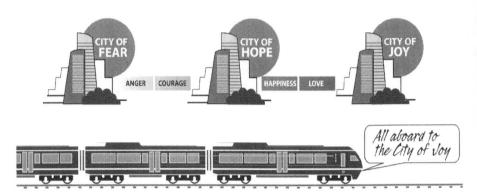

Illustration 34 - *Journey Through Your Emotions*

As you will appreciate by now, you won't get anywhere by resisting you, your negativity and your life, because you just keep receiving the same thing over and over again, caught up in the endless loop of learning, until you break the pattern. Also, the more you resist, the bigger the problem or challenge becomes. Choose to change your vibrational frequency because:

What you absolve dissolves

Absolve means to forgive and release. *Dissolve* means to end. So you've only got to get the learning once and then you are done! You never have to learn it again. By working with your Ego, forgiving you and those that caused you pain in the past, you will release the negative energies that have kept you stuck, or continue to sabotage your success.

Celebrate your success

As you become more and more aware, it is so important that you celebrate your success! Too many times people achieve something special and just move onto the next thing. When you feel that you have achieved something worth celebrating, celebrate in style.

Here are a few examples to whet your appetite:

- **Have afternoon lunch "alfresco"**
- **Go for a picnic in the park**
- **Drink champagne and eat strawberries**
- **Walk along the beach with a friend or loved one**
- **Buy tickets to your favorite play or musician**
- **Get your picture taken by a professional photographer**
- **Watch the sunset by candlelight**
- **Walk barefoot in the grass and make fists with your feet**
- **Buy yourself something luxurious**
- **Have an ice cream**

So, it is time to learn and give you something to celebrate!

The following exercise is about putting the first three truths into action. You will be spending time with you getting to know you, listening to your wants and needs, and going into the resistance.

EXERCISE 11

Going Into the Resistance

When you experience negative:

- **Self talk e.g. "I am not good enough"**

- **Feelings and emotions e.g. fear, anxiety**

- **Behavior that distracts you from something important like procrastination e.g. watching TV**

This is your Ego giving you an opportunity to learn a lesson and it's seeking to move you closer to joy.

So what are your lessons?

Use the table below or copy it into a notebook or onto a piece of paper and write as many things down in under Step 1 as you can. One thing per row.

Then complete Step 2. Step 2 is an opportunity for you to privately own and be responsible for your negativity.

The more things you write down under Steps 1 and 2, the more likely you will be able to identify a theme or pattern for you to learn from.

STEP 1.	STEP 2.
I want to be, enjoy my life, share with and receive...	But, the truth is... I am afraid that... *Insert negative self-talk, feelings, emotions and behaviors that hold you back.*
E.g. To run my own business	*E.g. I may fail. Also I don't want to look stupid to others, so it is easier to do nothing. I am afraid that I may not be taken seriously. I don't have the qualifications or the experience, etc.*

In the box below, write down the themes you have identified from Steps 1 and 2 above.

Then move onto Steps 3 and 4.

139

STEP 3. Who will I be in the world when this block does not exist and I have learned from my Ego?	STEP 4. Why do I want to get the learning and release this block?
E.g. An inspirational speaker, author, a successful business owner who inspires others to follow their hearts, embrace their natural talents and do what they love as a career.	*E.g. To experience joy every day, to be a role model, to lead by example, to look back on my life and know I helped others make a difference in their lives.*

Then move onto Steps 5 and 6.

STEP 5.	STEP 6.
What action do I need to take to learn from my ego, to release this block and move forward in my life?	**My daily mantra** *Making it hard to re-experience my negative behavior*
E.g. Every day I will consciously love the gifts and talents that I have. I will change my eating habits to be healthier and have more energy	*E.g. I am free to take care of myself and others; I always do what I say I am going to do.* *E.g. My accomplishments belong to me.* *E.g. I openly receive love into all aspects of my life*

Your actions will need a plan.

In the table below set out the action that you intend to work on that will enable you to start experiencing the very best of you.

When considering each action think about your commitment to yourself on a scale of 1 to 10. 1 being "I am not at all committed", 10 being "Bring it on!!!" This will give you some perspective about whether it should be in your Action Plan or not.

The number 1 rule is to get specific on your actions!

REMEMBER!

- **Your Action Plan is entirely about YOU and YOUR LIFE. If you lie or cheat you are only lying and cheating yourself!**

- **The actions you will complete with ease are those that will give you a resounding 10!**

- **In the beginning, make it easy for yourself. Start off by taking baby steps and build from there.**

My "Daily" Action points	Completion Date	Commitment on a scale of 1 to 10
E.g. For Health & Fitness - *Find a plan I can do daily that can travel with me and help me gain fitness and lose weight* *Complete plan daily and track my progress.* *Find an eating plan that I can follow and build into my daily routine easily.* *Plan my food shopping / discuss with my wife to make sure we are all on board.* *Find supporters to encourage me and kick my ass if needed (give them permission to do so).*	Next 7 days	10

TRUTH 4 – *What is yours will come to you*

The core lesson is…
Let go. Detach. Feel the relief first!

Wow! What a truth that is! Just knowing that should bring you massive relief, but I know from personal experience letting go, detaching and surrendering is harder than it seems because it requires massive trust - in you, in your spiritual self, in Source energy and in the divine spiritual system - that it will actually deliver!

Pause for a moment! If I said you have to let go of your heart's desire, the most important thing that you perceive is missing in your life, and potentially never receive it, notice what goes on inside – how is your Ego reacting? What thoughts are showing up? What feelings and emotions are you experiencing?

Or are you calm, serene, and completely okay with it? This is in fact where you need to get to, but when I ask clients the same question, typically their responses include… "You've got to be joking? I can't do that! I will never do that!" The feelings and emotions they experience are anxiety, frustration, anger, and even a feeling of sickness and loss.

When things go our way we are happy. But, when we allow ourselves to become attached to someone or something, and things don't go our way it causes us to panic because we are not only emotionally attached to the someone or something; we are also emotionally attached to the outcome we want to achieve. We react with such negative intensity about not getting what we want that we become accustomed to experiencing these emotions and we believe our lives will always be marked by the same outcomes of not getting what we want. And guess what? Because that is what we send out into The Web, that is exactly what we receive.

On a physical level, we continue to consolidate the same negative neural pathways that are wired together and fire together.

The reason for this is that the ego has a perception of control and when things don't go our way, we react because we feel it is outside our control – which it is.

Here is the distinction that you need to understand. *When you are attached to an outcome, you are not allowing yourself to actually receive it.* You are instead focusing on the control of what the outcome should look like and when you expect to receive it. You cannot possibly determine the timing of anything. Some outcomes will show up quickly, others will take time. There are an infinite number of factors that affect the timing of an outcome.

All you can do is take the appropriate course of action and ensure your thoughts, your feelings, your emotions, your self-talk and your behaviors are all aligned to the outcome you desire. When you do this and you are aligned, Source energy often brings you this or something better!

What if you could receive what is yours and not experience the negative reaction? That does not mean giving lip service to letting go, but instead arriving at a place you know it is already done, where you experience the relief now and accept with joy in your heart the outcome, which may not be what you first intended, but something even better. When you can do that magic happens!

You must learn to detach, let go, and surrender! Hand it over to Source energy and allow Source energy to create it for you, like your favorite meal, being created by the best chef in the world.

Detachment does not mean that you don't care. It means that you can focus and flow energy to what matters most. Detachment is the first step in the process of release. Cut the rope (Detach); drop the rope (Let Go), step to the side and trust (Surrender).

Detach, letting go and surrender is like throwing a boomerang, knowing it will *always* come back to you – sometimes it will be the same boomerang, other times it will be even better. If you know that it will always come back, experience the feelings of receiving that outcome in your life now. Send that vibration into The Web.

To help with letting go, you can focus on the symbol of the rune Ehwaz.

Ehwaz

Ehwaz is the rune of movement and progress. Focus on the symbol of Ehwaz to help with movement and progress of changes, new places, new attitudes, new dwellings or a new life. This can include developing new ideas, growing a business, or a relationship that needs to undergo change. As you cultivate your self, all else follows. What is yours will come to you.

146

TRUTH 5 – *Speaking highly of yourself will naturally change your results*

> **The core lesson is...**
> *Language has energy and power.*
> *Think before you speak.*

The words you use to describe your impact on how you show up day to day. Therefore it is so important that you choose words to help you feel better about yourself. Consequently the quality of your self-talk and the way you communicate with you, and about you, will determine the quality of your life experience and also shape the future life you design for yourself.

Often in life the opinion people hold of themselves is formed by other people's judgments and what they think about them. Accordingly, we allow our lives to become shaped by others. A lot of our energy is then spent living up to other people's expectations of us rather than what we want for ourselves. This is an act of self-sabotage and shows up in the stories we tell ourselves and in the masks that we wear.

I have heard my clients many times talk modestly about achievements and be self-critical. Putting ourselves down or underplaying our successes is considered in society to be humble and a way to earn the respect and approval of others.

Your level of achievement in life is directly proportionate to how you see yourself, which to be clear, is the opinion you hold about you. If you say that you are not worthy of respect, or not worthy of love or success, you will prove this to be true. If you choose to improve your opinion of yourself, you will develop the confidence to set higher goals, and you will actually achieve them.

Furthermore, who you say you are has an impact on your thoughts, your feelings, your behaviors and affects every part of your life. If you say you are not good enough, or not worthy or not capable, or not confident, then you will never take the first step. If you say you can, and you speak highly of yourself, you will naturally propel yourself towards the successful outcomes you desire. Although, a word of caution, don't go over the top and be egotistical – that would be ironic – because that can turn people off you, but you do want to get comfortable speaking confidently and truthfully about you e.g. you bake great novelty cakes, or you are a great speaker, or a great parent.

By changing the way you talk about yourself, will also change your physiology i.e. the way you hold your body, you will walk more confidently, talk more confidently and show up more confidently; as a result your actions and behaviors will change. It will also change your outlook on your life, the risks you are willing to take, the goals to pursue and the results you achieve.

The words you use have so much energy and power. They will either maintain your existing story or literally begin to write a new and updated story. Furthermore, like your thoughts, feelings, emotions, etc. they attract matching situations, circumstances and people into your life. So choose wisely.

Once you can uphold a positive image of you with confidence, the world will accept the same description of you, too.

Great Things about Me!

Write down as many great things about who you are and what you love about yourself.

I am...

I am...

I am...

I am...

I am...

I am...

I am...

I am...

I am...

I am...

I am...

I am...

I am...

I am...

I am...

I am...

I am...

I am...

EXERCISE 12

TRUTH 6 – *Your environment will enable you to flourish or falter*

The core lesson is...
Life conditions and environments contribute to your success.

Ask yourself the question:

"Will my current environment enable me and my life to flourish or falter?"

Flourish means that it will be nurtured, supported and it will grow healthily and exponentially.

Falter means it causes you to stumble, experience delays, lose confidence and begin to fail.

This truth is particularly important as you start the journey to your truth because you need to know where you are today, in the here and now, to help you understand where you want to progress to.

In the beginning, it is essential to regularly review your external environment to see what changes you can make or quick wins you can implement early on, to support you and help you grow e.g. to break bad habits or move away from bad relationships.

Even as your environment starts to change *naturally*, when you change your ways of thinking and your behaviors, it is still important to regularly pause to take stock on how far you have come and how well you have done. Then, appreciate your efforts, the changes you have made already and celebrate your successes. This will also give you the opportunity to tweak or make further changes as you move closer towards the life you want to live.

150

My Environment

Considering any and all of the following - your home, your workplace, your family, your friends, your health, your weight, the food you eat, how and where you spend your playtime - plus anything else that is important to you.

Answer the following question:

"Will my home, my workplace, my family, my friends, my health, my weight, my food, my play time enable me and my life to flourish?"

For each one, give it a score on a scale of 1 to 10 (1 = No never, and 10 = Yes absolutely). Please be honest with yourself. Remember if you lie or cheat you are only lying and cheating yourself.

For each score of less than 10, ask yourself what action you need to take to move from your current score e.g. 4 to a 10.

Then make a plan and take the action you choose. In the beginning this may be tricky, because you may need to start changing friends and social circles, so be gentle with yourself and your life, take small steps and make small changes that suit your needs. As one change embeds, move onto the next and so on.

Why is your environment so important?

Imagine you have a favorite, colorful fish that loves swimming around in its fish bowl. Unfortunately, you cannot see its beautiful colors because it has become so dirty, swimming around a dirty fish bowl. You decide to take your fish out of the bowl and clean it, but you forget to clean the bowl as well. When you put your clean fish back into its dirty environment (the fish bowl), it becomes dirty again very quickly.

In other words, as you get to know you and start to design a life that will fulfil you, if you don't continue to clean your environment internally i.e. by learning from your negative self- talk, thoughts, feelings, emotions, actions, and behaviors, and externally e.g. your physical surroundings and your relationships, eventually, like the fish, you will become dirty again. You will experience the ***elastic band effect*** and snap back into the old ways and old patterns.

So consistency is key.

Othala

Othala is the rune of separation and separating paths. Focus on the symbol of Othala when you need to shed old skins by changing your environment. This can include discarding outmoded relationships, changes to your home, career, health, personal habits or old conditioning that has previously held you back.

Your Peer Group

Your Peer Group is a fundamental part of your life and your environment.

*A **Peer Group** is a social group of people who have similar interests, age, background and social status, i.e. the people who you choose to spend your time with.*

Your Peer Group, is a direct reflection of your environment and who you are in the here and now. They are attracted to you by your Ego and will either help you or hinder you in your life.

152

Therefore, who you choose to spend your time with also contributes to your success. So choose wisely.

Yes, you can consciously choose your peer group and I invite you to do so. But, in life, we don't normally do this. Instead we tend to just go with the flow and hang out with people we don't get along with or sometimes even like. We say "yes" to going out somewhere, because we don't want to look bad, or hurt someone else's feelings. So instead we hurt ourselves by going into environments that don't serve us at the highest level. How amazing would it be to spend time with people whose company you enjoy and always make you happy? Your time is precious and should be appreciated by all those people you choose to share it with, including you. Choose to become more aware about who you spend your time with and why you spend your time with them. Use what follows to help you.

A Poor Peer Group...

● **May compel you to do something you dislike, something that you will be unhappy doing. And more often than not, you won't succeed. Succumbing to the opinions of others, especially in making important decisions in your life will only lead to regret. For example, choosing a career just because your friends did so without much thought about your interests and talents will only make you unhappy. How do I know? Because this was me. My first career was in banking and my second career was in accounting. Both choices I made were a direct result of other people's opinions about what they thought I should do. For the first 10 years of my working life I was unhappy and unfulfilled!**

- May lead to you adopting a certain kind of lifestyle, bad habits that keep you stuck in the past and worse, still a loss of your individuality. E.g., it may lead you to follow blindly what your peers feel and say is right. You adopt their tastes in fashion, clothing, hair, music and lifestyle. At an extreme, you may lose your own taste. You may feel forced to like what they like or do what they do and join the bandwagon; you lose your originality of thought and conduct. You forget the way you wanted to live. You lose your identity.

On the other hand, **Great Peer Groups...**

- Can be incredibly loving, caring and supportive.

- Can help you reflect on yourself, teach you good things and encourage you to follow your dreams. They may inspire you, motivate you, and help you change for the better. Looking at what others do can help you bring positive changes in your ways of thinking, your actions and your behaviors. If you choose the right people to spend your time with, they can push you towards something positive and help you adopt great habits in your life, e.g. seeing that some of your friends exercise daily, may cause you to do the same.

- Can actually expose you to new ways of being in the world, e.g. their choices, what they think about in life, how they perceive situations, how they react in different circumstances.

- Can help you and lead you to making better choices for you in your life.

- **Can influence the shaping of your personality in a positive way when you choose the right kind of people who support you in your life. Their perspective of life can lead you to change yours, e.g. your peers can inspire you to become more optimistic or more confident. Your peers may influence you to change and make you a better human being.**

I call my peer group, my community of unconditional love and trust. I feel completely safe to be me. There is never any judgment of me, but that does not mean they don't call me out when my head disappears up my backside on occasion. They help me to see me and realign to my truth.

A member of my peer group recently said that he measured who he spends his time with based on three things… *Are they kind, do they care and do they make you laugh?*

My Peer Group

Reflecting on the above, consider how you will now choose your peer group and do the people in your current peer group still qualify?

If you have never done this exercise before, now is the time to do it as the quality of your peer group will affect your life!

EXERCISE 14

TRUTH 7 – *The more you love your life, the more your life will love you*

The core lesson is...

Love your life with a passion!

Fully play out your life and live at 100 degrees!

I have heard people say that they give 100% in all they do, but can't understand why they have not yet achieved their goals or are living their dreams. When this happens my response is the same – "What are you focusing your energy on and are you being true to yourself?", because something they are sending out into The Web is stopping them from reaching their goal.

This truth invites you to live with passion. Water boils *naturally* at 100 degrees. When you watch water boil, the energy is abundant, vigorous, passionate and focused, but at 99 degrees the water is just hot.

You can give 100% at 99 degrees and live a good life, or you can give 1% at 100 degrees and live an even better life.

What would happen if you gave 100% at 100 degrees? This is what people do when they consistently live in their intuitive truth and focus their energy into what they love and what they are passionate about.

The more you are passionate about your life, the more your life will be passionate about you, and the bigger the returns will be for you to enjoy. When you live in this energy, the Web sends you exactly the same back, over and over and over and over again!

Enjoying What I Love!

This is a very important exercise. Take time to answer ALL the following questions in ALL three parts.

PART 1

Reflecting on all the aspects of your life, your home, your work, your friends, your family, your health, your wealth, etc. What do you love to enjoy in your life? What are you passionate about? How do you like to pamper yourself? What treats do you give yourself?

PART 2

How do you feel when you do something you are passionate about or when you pamper yourself or when you give yourself a treat? What is your energy like? What is your physiology like i.e. what do you do with your body, how do you walk, how do you move? What sorts of things do you say to yourself before, during and after? What is your outlook on life like during and after? What do you feel like you can achieve? How do you treat other people?

PART 3

How do your answers to the above questions compare to the questions in Exercise 1 that you completed at the beginning of this book?

Knowing what you now know, what are you going to do more of and what are you going to do less of, to bring more passion into your life?

TRUTH 8– *There is always an opportunity for kindness*

*Those who bring sunshine to the lives of others
cannot keep it from themselves.*

~James Matthew Barrie

The core lesson is...

Love you completely and unconditionally!

No matter what you experience in your life, the only person that will remain *constant* is you, therefore it is so important to love you and be kind to you. Acts of kindness will raise your energy and will bring more peace and harmony into your life. Furthermore when you're willing to share your kindness, other people may be inspired by your example and think about doing something kind themselves.

Being kind to other people we care about is normal, it is part of human nature, but what does it mean to be kind to you? Here are a few ideas for you to enjoy.

First of all **be patient**. Especially as you embark on this journey *with you* to decipher your code. Sometimes, you will get it spot on absolutely perfect, other times, you will get frustrated or even irritated with yourself. Remember if you get frustrated with yourself, pay attention, because you will be reliving a past experience, but be careful not to get stuck there. Please be patient, allow yourself to naturally unfold in your own time, don't try to hurry up or to rush it. It will be worth it in the end. You are not in competition. Enjoy the process and enjoy you.

Share a smile with you. When you look in the mirror, express joy. Show yourself that you are happy with you, and that you make you happy.

Give yourself compliments. Tell yourself you look great today. Tell yourself how clever you are. Praise yourself for voicing your opinion or sharing your thoughts and feelings.

Show yourself respect. Be courteous to yourself. Stand up for you and say thank you when you have done something great for you.

Give yourself a boost. When things get tough, encourage yourself to keep going.

Be thoughtful about your needs. How many times do you wish someone else could have been more thoughtful towards you before they did something or said something? Give yourself the same gift.

Forgive. Forgiveness is not always easy, but if you get something really wrong please forgive yourself. Don't dwell on what could have been. Unburden yourself of the past and think kind thoughts again about you. Release the energy and let it go! You will be amazed at the ripple effect an ounce of forgiveness can have in your life.

Take time out. In life there will be ups and downs. When you feel tired, don't push through to please others. Listen to you and just stop. Give yourself the gift of rejuvenation because it is the key to success. Remember, you will not be able to give to others if you don't take care of you first.

Give yourself a treat. Treat yourself to what you love - maybe it's a day out with a loved one, or even a day out with you. Take yourself out to lunch, buy yourself some flowers, run yourself a hot bubble bath or relax and sit in the sunshine and feel the warmth on your face, listen to your favorite song and dance like no one is watching, or sing like no one is listening. Make giving yourself a treat easy and fun to do. Have some quick wins that don't take too long to fulfil so you can see, feel and hear the benefits straight away.

Send yourself a kind message. What do you love about you?

Expect nothing in return. The greatest acts of kindness are those that are freely given, because you care about you and want you to be happy. The amazing thing about kindness is that it will improve your sense of wellbeing and happiness.

Whatever you do in your life, do it with love and joy in your heart because when you share love or share joy with anyone, your body will fill with love and joy, so you get to feel it first!

The Journey to Your Truth

I ONCE said to someone the words *"I know that"* who then responded, *"Be careful, they are the three most dangerous words."* I found this response curious, but did not really pay any attention to it. Then shortly afterwards, I saw the same words being said on Facebook, with the same, what now appeared automatic, response – *"Be careful, they are the three most dangerous words."* Whenever, I see or hear or experience the same thing more than once, my whole being perks up to pay attention, because this is often a lesson for me to learn or for me to teach.

When I sat thinking about the phrase the response in my mind was "Surely that depends on whether it flows from a Belief system or a Truth system" and then what follows in this chapter came flooding through.

As you embark on the journey to your intuitive truth, to the future time when you have learned the lessons from your Ego and you are living the life you designed for yourself, you will have bounced back and forth through four different stages:

STAGE 1: The **Beliefs** you tell yourself

STAGE 2: What is **Known** to you

STAGE 3: The **Unknown**

STAGE 4: Your **Truth**

The Journey through the four stages is on the continuum you can see below:

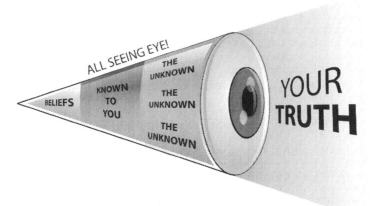

Illustration 35 - *The Journey to Your Truth*

In this chapter, I will briefly explain and share with you the essential foundation of each of the four stages that you need to work with your Ego's Code.

STAGE 1 – *The Beliefs you tell yourself*

What are beliefs?

The dictionary definition of "What is a belief" includes the following:

"Acceptance that something exists or is true, without proof"

"Feeling sure that something is true"

"Acceptance that a statement is true"

"An opinion"

The terms, "without proof", "feeling sure" "acceptance that" "an opinion" all lack clarity and certainty.

Consequently all four definitions create uncertainty because they are missing the key component - proof. This is also the case in life. In particular, the beliefs that hold you back lack certainty and proof to back them up. Consequently they cause you to experience all forms of negativity such as doubt, worry, anxiety and fear. Consider the following beliefs:

"I'm not good enough; Money hates me; I don't have the experience; Everyone will laugh at me; I am unlovable; Nobody listens to me; They will just say 'no', so what's the point? I'm invisible; my feelings don't matter; what I think is stupid; I can't be me; I will be rejected; I'm not confident."

All of the above are examples of distortions, perceptions, assumptions and judgments that we have made or placed upon ourselves.

You will recall my Claytonism from earlier - *the second you judge yourself; you lose all ability to influence and impact your life* – it is exactly the same for the distortions, perceptions and assumptions you make about you.

> A *distortion* is a misleading account or impression we have.
>
> A *perception* is the way something is regarded or interpreted.
>
> An *assumption* is something that is accepted as true, without proof.
>
> A *judgment* is a decision that we have made rightly or wrongly.

In other words, they are the *lies* that we tell ourselves. If you look at the word belief, it shows you exactly what it is: Be-**LIE**-f.

I need to be careful here because some people have what they would call very strong positive beliefs that have served them and continue to serve them well e.g. a belief in faith, or a belief in God or a belief in the Divine. I do not consider this to be a belief as I have described above; this would be something that you will have seen deliver a result or experienced for yourself and so would be in Stage 2 – What is known to you, which I will go through shortly.

All your beliefs are past driven from your current life and your past lives. Furthermore, all beliefs have a low energetic vibration, which is why they can cause you to become closed, retreat from life, lose self-esteem, and lose confidence in yourself or your ability. They can further impact on your coping skills, hinder or lower your immune system and increase the likelihood of stress.

Remember, I said that beliefs operate on a continuum. Of course there are things you know you cannot do *yet*; talents and gifts that you are *yet* to discover; learning you are *yet* to learn. If you are closed to your Ego and continue to ignore or avoid or stuff down your negativity, then your beliefs will remain the lies that you tell yourself every day, and you will remain stuck exactly where you are in the **endless loop of negative learning.**

What Are the Lies (be-LIE-f's) I Tell Myself?

In this box, write down all the beliefs you tell yourself about yourself, your skills, your relationships, and your life - that hold you back

_____

_____

_____

_____

_____

_____

_____

_____

EXERCISE 16

For each belief, ask yourself the question, "What is my truth in this situation?" Your Higher Self must and will always reply with your truth. Having raised your awareness to your old beliefs, when they show up practice replacing them then with your more empowering truth.

If you want to go one step further, ask yourself the question, "What behavior is my truth in this situation?" Again, your Higher Self must and will always reply with your truth. When your old beliefs show up, practice replacing them with your new, more empowering behaviors.

STAGE 2 – *What is known to you*

As you move along the continuum, being open to new ideas, and new experiences, you will enjoy more of your life, learn new skills, gain new knowledge to practice and embed. The more you gain practical experience by applying what you have learned the easier it will become for you to master (New Know-How). When it becomes natural, instinctive and part of your being, it will then be known to you. In other words it is something that you can *own, now*.

Again, when you look at the word Known, it shares with you its true divine meaning...

Kn-**own,** K-**now**-n

When your new know-how is positive and you start to own it, it can be a springboard to move you forward into the next stage – The Unknown.

However, if the evidence you experience in your life is negative and consolidates your old belief, because of the way people continue to treat you, or because of the results you continue to get, you could give it a negative meaning e.g. Why does this keep happening to me?, consequently it could be incapacitating. This is because the trauma of the past is not yet fully healed, moving you back down the continuum to continue learning.

I have also seen people not own the positive evidence before them, because of other beliefs they have going on. Even though they have the proof that they can be a great father, a greater teacher, a great speaker, a great author or entrepreneur, they don't accept the confirming proof in front of them. Their belief systems dismiss it, call it a fluke or freak of nature. As a result, they then move back down the continuum to learn more about the beliefs they tell themselves.

This only happens if there are other things for you to learn. You may find on your journey to your intuitive truth that you move back and forth for a while between your beliefs and what is known to you.

Perseverance is key. You need to keep practicing and embedding your new knowledge until it becomes instinctive. Your past life and current life traumas will eventually heal and go away. Your past does not have to equal your future. You can design and live your dream life free from the negativity and the traumas of your past. The more past negative energy you heal and release, the happier you will become. The changes to your neural pathways will start to take place now, not just in the future, so the more you honor you, spend time with you, take care of you, change your thoughts, change your behaviors, your feelings will change, your self-talk will change, your personality will change and so will the reality you call your life. You will start seeing evidence straight away, not some time in the distant future.

What is known to you, is on the edge of now (k-now-n) and the Unknown, which brings us to Stage 3.

STAGE 3 – *The Unknown*

You cannot see the unknown from your beliefs or the known. You can only dream about it or imagine what it will be like. It is the space between the now and your truth. It is what you are becoming. It is like "no man's land." It is the place that you start to embed new decisions that you have made, new ideals and standards you set for yourself, the identity you see for yourself, and the life that you are designing.

It is not the now; it is beyond the now. It is the **Un-Now**.

Again when you look at the word, it shares with you its true divine meaning - the

Un-K-now-n. It is where the magic truly happens.

For a while you may bounce back and forth between the known and the unknown as you truly get to know you and design the life you want to live.

On a physical level, science and biology support the idea that we can change the brain by thought alone, so that your brain looks like a future reality has already happened. Therefore, it must follow that you can train your brain to accept that the future reality in your **Unknown** as if it is happening now. As a result, you can create new neural pathways that wire and fire together, sending out a new higher vibrational frequency from your Ego and Higher Self. This in turn frees the true you in all your magnificence and attracts the life experience your true heart desires into your here and now.

STAGE 4 – *Your Truth*

This is your Unified Being embedded into your Realm of Fulfilment. Your cornucopia! Your utopia!

Imagine how that would feel. Imagine what that would look like compared to where you are today. Who are you? How would you describe yourself? Who would you be sharing your life with? Where would you be living? What would you be doing for a career? If you could take a blank sheet of paper and draw it, what would you draw?

So, how do you know if you are living in your intuitive truth? If you recall, there will not be any RUTS (t-rut-h) in your life. Whenever there is a problem in your life that does not feel good, or it feels like something is blocking your path and you experience negativity of any kind, you are in a RUT, and if you are in a RUT you are not in your truth, and if you are not in truth you are not in unity. It is at this point you need to raise your awareness and pay attention because you are reliving your past and have something to learn.

On your journey to your intuitive truth, you need to know the following:

- **You will move up and down the continuum. This is normal.**

- **You cannot be in the first two stages at the same time with the same learning.**

- **You can only be in the first two stages at the same time with different pieces of learning because they flow through Linear Time, i.e. you learn one piece of knowledge, before you move onto the next.**

> **What is Linear Time?** *Linear time is when time flows in a horizontal straight line from past to present to the future.*

In Linear Time, things take longer to create because you physically use your body to take action, to make a change or to learn something new.

Whereas when you are in stages 3 and 4 you are connected to all things everywhere, at the same time. You are experiencing Temporal Timelessness where time, space and matter are all rolled into one and happening simultaneously - you have become one with all there is.

In Temporal Timelessness your manifestation **comes to you**. You do not go in search for it.

In essence when you live in your truth your energy vibration is a vibrational match to your hearts desires and so changes in your life manifest a lot quicker, sometimes instantaneously.

● **You will experience glimpses of your truth and of your Ego-free identity as your new life begins to appear.**

Illustration 36 shows the four key stages of the Journey to Your Truth as discussed above.

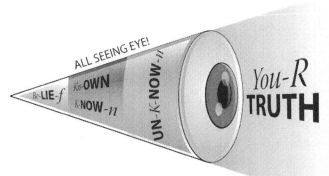

Illustration 36 - *The Journey to Your Truth - Key Stages*

Finally, your journey will be very special and very relevant to where you are in your life right now, so embrace it and embrace you.

Give yourself the gift of YOU and live a life that is true to who you really are!

PART THREE:

LIVING YOUR TRUTH

- CREATING THE NEW YOU!

Understand the truth behind your negativity!

Learn how to decipher your code…
…and stop sabotaging your success!

Living Your Truth

Be You

The exercises in this book will help you to build a solid foundation of being you. When you have that solid foundation, you have established your own sense of identity. So, no matter what happens in your life, what curve balls are thrown or what joy you experience, you will always know exactly who you are. There may be times when you may feel lost in the wilderness or unfocused and distracted, but if you know who you are, you'll be able to get back on track.

Be Focused

As we have discussed many times, when you live in flow and from a place of Unified Being you are always being yourself. You are then more likely to have clearer focus in your life and a clearer direction for your life.

When you stay true to who you are, you are more likely to know the goals you want to achieve and more importantly how to want to go about achieving them. You are then able to stay focused and know which direction to take to give yourself the greatest opportunity for success.

Be Congruent

There is a direct correlation between how you feel, your performance and your results in life, i.e. the happier you feel, the better your performance, the better your results.

The truth is that your immediate and long-term success is directly linked to your happiness and quality of life and this is driven by how congruent you are.

Being congruent and being yourself means living your life in alignment with your values. When you are not yourself, you could take on the values and ideals of others that do not serve you. When you know your values and why you do what you do, you will live according to your own truth. Use Exercises 3 and 9 to help you.

Be Courageous

Have the courage to be different. Consistently living your truth is a courageous journey because there will always be people in life who don't see the world as you do and as a result will challenge the way you choose to live your life.

As you embark on your journey you may have to do things in the beginning you don't want to do e.g., working in a job that you have outgrown, but it could take time before you find another job that meets your needs. Until then, every day may be a challenge and potentially a negatively charged environment. What will you do in such circumstances? How will you stay true to who you are?

It takes a great amount of courage to decide to take the path that goes against the crowd. The reason why the majority of people take the easy road is because it's easy. It's easier to just follow the crowd as opposed to find your own way. It's more of a challenge when you stay true to yourself and live your life your way. This challenge of always being yourself takes courage and inner strength. No matter what comes your way, you'll know how to handle it.

Be Well

When living your truth it is so important to take care of you every day because you need energy to enjoy you and your life to the full. This means living a healthy lifestyle. For example, drink 8 glasses of water each day, eat healthy foods, move your body through regular exercise that you enjoy, get 8 hours sleep, and above all else laugh, play and have fun. Find out what is best and right for you and then stick to it.

If you don't take care of yourself, you could become tired and irritable. Tiredness and a tired body is the Ego's playground. In this situation you could experience rapid and overwhelming learning.

There are many different types of playgrounds, because there are different levels of tiredness. When you get tired you can experience anything from "I just can't be bothered" to "overwhelm" to "self sabotage." It is in this state that your Ego can appear destructive. What is actually happening is your ability to keep things hidden, consciously or unconsciously fades and disappears, and so the Ego show must go on!

Your resistance is limited because you are so tired and you often find yourself in situations before you feel you are ready.

However, remember one golden rule: your divine spiritual self will never bring you anything you cannot handle. Just remember the five steps:

STEP 1: *Pay attention!*

STEP 2: *Acknowledge and show appreciation
for the reaction!*

STEP 3: *Your awareness and acknowledgement creates
presence, which temporarily moves you from the
past into the here and now.*

STEP 4: *From the 'here and now' make a choice – are you
going to react or respond?*

STEP 5: *Having made your choice, take appropriate action.*

Be *"The Change"*

"Be the change you want to see in the world" is a famous saying by Gandhi. To live your truth, you must "Be the change you want to see in your life."

You cannot force joy or happiness into your life, it comes from within and must be nurtured to grow and flourish. However, to make changes big or small it can mean sacrifice, discipline and hard work which can all seem daunting, overwhelming, create doubt and cause us to stay still in what we already know. But if we want to make a change, it is often because we are unhappy with the current situation in some way. The best way to make any change is to give yourself permission.

Granting yourself permission allows you to be who you are and also to acknowledge who you want to be. You do not need to be perfect and the situation does not need to be perfect to give yourself permission. Giving yourself permission shifts your mindset from what you think you should do, maybe for other people, to choosing what is right for you. Giving yourself permission opens up your mind to endless possibilities and allows your choices to thrive.

In all that you are, and all that you want to become, give yourself permission.

Be Free

What follows is a brilliant, quick and easy visual to keep you on track and stop you living in the past. I came across this theory when I was working in Denmark with a friend. I have updated and adapted it for the Ego's Code and to help you live in your truth.

To be free you must choose to live above the line!

Living above line means you spend your time enjoying your life, a life full of love, a life full of choices and endless possibilities. You have a sense of purpose and live what truly makes your heart sing. You have left your past behind you and instead of living there you use your past challenges as a reference library to help you in life. You constantly feel joyful, connected, focused, energized, happy, grounded, grateful, confident and fulfilled.

To live below the line means you continue to relive your past. You will be consumed in drama, challenges, problems and excuses that have always haunted you. Living below the line means you ignore your negativity, stuff it down, avoid opportunities to learn, blame others when things don't go right for you and ultimately give up. It often leaves you feeling frustrated, angry, fearful, defeated, resentful and anxious.

So where do you choose to live your life? Use the following illustration to help you day to day stay in your truth:

Illustration 37 - *Living Above the Line*

Be Grateful

Gratitude is the appreciation of your truth
and the truth of others

- Clayton John Ainger

Show appreciation and express gratitude every day!

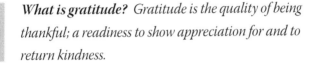 *What is gratitude?* *Gratitude is the quality of being thankful; a readiness to show appreciation for and to return kindness.*

People tend to take for granted the good and great that is already present in their lives. Studies have shown that expressing gratitude can increase your well-being, your quality of life and your happiness by as much as 25%.

(Source: Counting Blessings Versus Burdens, Emmons & McCullough, 2003).

There are two kinds of gratitude I invite you to express:

1. **Notice and appreciate the gifts you receive each and every day. Write down three things you are grateful for about you, in your life and for others who share your life, for those who teach you, for simple pleasures and for all that you receive.**

2. **For your future life. Gratitude is an emotion expressing appreciation for what is already done. When you express gratitude for the future and the unknown you are signaling to your physical body, to your divine self and to Source energy that it is already done and already here. Then watch the magic unfold.**

A Final Truth

"Everybody is talented, original and has something important to say"

- Brenda Ueland

You have a story to tell – share your story with others!

Appendices:
My Values Exercise

STEP 1
Write down 20 things that are important to you in your life e.g. family, friends, money, music, dancing, learning, etc.

1 _____

2 _____

3 _____

4 _____

5 _____

6 _____

7 _____

8 _____

9 _____

10 _____

11 _____

12 _____

13 _____

14 _____

15 _____

16 _____

17 _____

18 _____

19 _____

20 _____

Out of the above list, write down the first thing on your list in the box below e.g. family.

```



```

STEP 2: *My feelings*

In the box below, write down **three positive** feelings or emotions this thing enables you to feel and enjoy in your life.

1 _____

2 _____

3 _____

STEP 3: *What else is important to you?*

From **Step 1**, write down the next **four** things in your life that are important to you. As for Step 2, write opposite three positive feelings or emotions these things enable you to enjoy in your life.

Important Thing	Three positive feelings or emotions
1	
2	
3	
4	

STEP 4: *What else, what else, what else?*

Using the remainder of the things that are important to you from **Step 1**, complete the table on the following page. Again, write down three feelings or emotions for each of the important things in your life. It's OK to repeat feelings for different, important aspects.

Important Thing	Three positive feelings or emotions
1	
2	
3	
4	
5	
6	
7	
8	

Important Thing	Three positive feelings or emotions
9 _____	_____
	_____
	_____
10 _____	_____
	_____
	_____
11 _____	_____
	_____
	_____
12 _____	_____
	_____
	_____
13 _____	_____
	_____
	_____
14 _____	_____
	_____
	_____
15 _____	_____
	_____
	_____

STEP 5: *Review your values*

For each feeling or emotion that you value from **Steps 2, 3** and **4**, write them down on a small piece of paper. ONE feeling or emotion per piece of paper and then put them into one pile. Take your pile of values and then sub-divide them into two piles:

MUST HAVES
"I cannot and will not live without them in my life"
NICE TO HAVES

Then place the "Nice to Haves" to one side. *Please note*, they are important to you, but they are not core to who you are.

STEP 6: *My Value Groupings*

In your 'Must Have' values there may be values that mean similar things to you. Take your Must Have values and sort them in groups of similar values and then assign a Core Value to each group that would describe all the other values in that group. It is really important for you to split your values into between six and eight core groups to make it easier for you to work with them in your life. Then in the table below write your core values in the left hand column and in the central column list the values that are similar.

The next part of **Step 7** is to prioritize your values. When you prioritize your core values, it is important for you to compare each value to each other. The way that you do this is as per the example below.

Here is the story I share with participants when I help them prioritize their values on my events. Imagine your six core values are love, integrity, growth, security, joy and freedom. Congratulations, you have won a vacation! You have packed two suitcases – love and integrity. You get to the check-in desk at the airport, but you are told you can only take one case with you. Which is most important? Love or integrity? For the important core value you assign one point. Then you compare love to growth, love to security, love to joy and love to freedom assigning a point to the value you choose as the priority. This is love done.

You then move onto integrity. You compare integrity to growth, integrity to security, integrity to joy, and integrity to freedom, again assigning a point to the value that you choose as the priority.

After you have completed this for all your core values, you add up the scores and prioritize them at **Step 7**.

Core Value	Similar values in my group	Prioritization

STEP 7: *My prioritized values*

Having sorted your values into their priority order, please record them in the table below with the most important ones first.

Order	Core Value
1	
2	
3	
4	
5	
6	
7	
8	

STEP 8: *My behaviors for honoring my values*

Repeat **Exercise 3** on page 44, which we covered in **Part 1** for each of your core values. Please record as much behavior as possible that will ensure you live and honor your values every day with integrity! Set yourself up to WIN! The more you live your values the easier they will be, from being intellectually operational to instinctively natural and normal.

VALUE 1

_____

_____

_____

_____

_____

_____

_____

_____

VALUE 2

_____

_____

_____

_____

_____

_____

_____

_____

VALUE 3

VALUE 4

VALUE 5

VALUE 6

VALUE 7

VALUE 8

About the Author

CLAYTON PLAYS many roles in his life, the most important to him is being a dad and husband.

Clayton is a very passionate individual. He is passionate about loving life and enjoying every aspect of it. His ethos in life is about making every person matter every time. This is why he is so passionate about people and helping them to embrace their individuality, and understand the power of doing what comes naturally and discover what truly makes their hearts sing!

Clayton and his wife Lindsay run a successful training and consultancy business working with people all over the world, from different walks of life. From once being a tax specialist Clayton is now a sought-after consultant and speaker on "Why people don't do better, when they know better."

Clayton loves to be different, to challenge the status quo, and inspire the people and companies he works with to explore new ways of thinking, attitudes and behaviors, transforming lives and results for the long-term.

Clayton is also a spiritual teacher, psychic medium and shamanic healer. The Ego's Code is a culmination of Clayton's spiritual journey so far. This is his passion – helping people, like you, to embrace your true self and supporting you in living what truly makes your heart sing!

How best to describe Clayton comes from the people who have worked with him.

"A meeting with Clayton is like finding the right key to your inner self. It is said that 'Clarity is power' so find your clarity and get the tools to connect with your self on a deeper level. Clayton has totally taken the 'mystical' out of the spiritual for me. I enjoy the benefits every day. The peace and acceptance is making my every day a joyful one."

"I was able to heal a totally battered, unloved and broken heart. I realized I have been afraid to live my truth because of the true power that I am, but in hiding this I am not being true to me or what the true me can bring to all I meet. Thank you."

"To finally feel that the missing pieces of me have fit back into place is the most amazing feeling. What Clayton brings is a gift beyond measure. The blessing received goes deep into one's very soul."

"Clayton's ability to bring passion to every aspect of life is highly contagious. With his enthusiasm and genius, Clayton inspires you to find the meaning that you can give to your life and how you can stay true to yourself. The most important journey you can take is the journey within – a journey to the truth of who you really are.

Bringing Clayton along on my journey has brought me deeper fulfilment because I have recaptured the key to the genius me. He has helped me to reconnect with my true self so that I can embrace my life with a fresh perspective and new energy."

Clayton's promise to you is this –

"I will help you grow beyond the boundaries of your perceived knowledge and capabilities, so that you achieve your true heart's desire."

Printed in Great Britain
by Amazon.co.uk, Ltd.,
Marston Gate.